FOR THE RECORD VI

STILL YET MORE ENCOURAGING WORDS FOR ORDINARY CATHOLICS

Rev. J. Ronald Knott

Sophronismos Press
Louisville, Kentucky

FOR THE RECORD VI
Still Yet More Encouraging Words for Ordinary Catholics

For information address:
Sophronismos Press
1271 Parkway Gardens Court #106
Louisville, Kentucky 40217.

First Printing: September 2008

ISBN 978-0-9800023-1-7

Also by J. Ronald Knott

BOOKS FOR CLERGY

Diocesan Priests in the Archdiocese of Louisville;
Archdiocese of Louisville Vocation Office, 2001

Religious Communities in the Archdiocese of Louisville;
Archdiocese of Louisville Vocation Office, 2002

INTENTIONAL PRESBYTERATES:
Claiming Our Common Sense of Purpose as Diocesan Priests;
(Spanish and Swahili editions available) Sophronismos Press, 2003

FROM SEMINARIAN TO DIOCESAN PRIEST:
Managing a Successful Transition;
(Spanish edition available) Sophronismos Press, 2004

THE SPIRITUAL LEADERSHIP OF A PARISH PRIEST:
On Being Good and Good At It;
(Spanish edition available) Sophronismos Press, 2007

INTENTIONAL PRESBYTERATES: *The Workbook;*
Sophronismos Press, 2007

A BISHOP AND HIS PRIESTS TOGETHER:
Resources for Building More Intentional Presbyterates;
Sophronismos Press, 2011

HOMILIES / SPIRITUALITY

AN ENCOURAGING WORD: *Renewed Hearts, Renewed Church;*
Sophronismos Press, 1995

ONE HEART AT A TIME:
Renewing the Church in the New Millennium;
Sophronismos Press, 1999

SUNDAY NIGHTS: *Encouraging Words for Young Adults;*
Sophronismos Press, 2000

FOR THE RECORD BOOK SERIES

FOR THE RECORD:
Encouraging Words for Ordinary Catholics, Volumes I - X;
Sophronismos Press 2003 - 2012

**For information about where to purchase eBook and
printed editions of Father Knott's books,
go to: www.ronknottbooks.com**

To my friends
MAREA, PATRICIA and JEAN

Acknowledgments

I would like to thank Mr. Joseph Duerr, editor of The Record, our archdiocesan newspaper, for giving me the opportunity to write these weekly columns. I also thank Mr. Glenn Rutherford for editing these columns each week and for giving me valuable advice along the way.

I would like to offer a special thanks to Ms. Lori Massey for further editing and also formatting these columns into a book and Tim Schoenbachler for preparing this Create Space edition. Last of all, I would like to thank the many supportive readers who have encouraged me to keep on writing and who have taken the time to let me know how much these words of encouragement have meant to them.

Table of Contents

Write down all these things that have happened to you.
TOBIT 12:20

When my first An Encouraging Word column was published, back in September 2002, I had no idea that I would still be writing it many years later. With this column, however, I am finishing my sixth year and beginning my seventh!

Thinking back, I had several reasons for doing this: (1) I wanted to encourage ordinary Catholics during the sexual abuse scandal that broke in early 2002. (2) For personal survival during those dark days, I wanted to make myself focus on the positive things that our Church has to offer. (3) Several people told me they missed my printed homilies after I had left the Cathedral. (4) Because of a very busy schedule, I was unable to say "yes" to a handful of individuals who had been asking me to be their spiritual director.

This column was my answer to all four of those situations. I wrote in that first column that this opportunity would give me a chance to "enlarge my pulpit." Has it ever! I know that 67,600 copies of The Record are circulated weekly. I don't know how many people in those families actually read this column, but I have anecdotal and hard evidence that there are many, many people who read it.

Hardly a day goes by that I do not run into people who stop me to tell me how much they enjoy reading this column. Regularly, I notice people staring at me from across parking lots, in stores or other public places. I used to think that something was wrong, but I have discovered that they are simply trying to remember where they have seen my face. It is always a nice experience when that moment of recognition comes and they speak.

These experiences have forced me to behave myself in public. I was recently getting off a plane, not in a very good mood, when three different readers stopped me.

Because I have put them in book form for convenience and further distribution, I know that they are being read by people in several states and even by a few people in a few foreign countries.

I have learned from this writing experience that there are many wonderful ordinary Catholics out there who enjoy my simple, straightforward messages of encouragement. Even though I honor and celebrate their work, I cannot write erudite books on spirituality and religion like Father George Kilcourse or even fascinating and informative historical works like Father Clyde Crews. They are both smarter than I will ever be, but it does appear that I have my own niche and my own readership – and for that I am grateful.

Finally, this writing has become such a familiar spiritual discipline for me that I would now find it hard to quit – so I won't!

All six volumes of *An Encouraging Word* are available at Maloney Center, Tonini's Church Goods, Marian Center and online at www.ronknottbooks.com or www.store.saintmeinrad.edu/scholarshop.

September 25, 2008

"They encouraged them to persevere in the faith."
ACTS 14:22

Finding God's Presence in the "Thin Places"

They say that our polluting ways have caused "holes" in the delicate ozone layer, which keeps us from being fried by the sun's radiation.

In the spiritual world, there are similar "holes" in the dense layer that veil our view of God. Instead of deadly rays from the sun, a little of God himself shines through.

The Irish call them "thin places," places where the separation between heaven and earth, the sacred and the secular, seems especially porous. God leaks through more easily in these places, it is thought. Another way of saying it is that, in such places, people find the presence of God more easily.

I, too, have been in such places where God seemed especially present.

Before she died at age 98, I used to fix a Mother's Day brunch every year for an old friend who was not even kin to me. It was always a magic time, a time when I felt that I was actually mediating God's love to someone who needed to feel it in a tangible way. On such occasions, it was obvious from her face that these simple gestures had great significance.

When I was on-call at the neonatal unit of Norton Hospital, I was called in the wee hours of the morning by the parents of a very sick child. When I got there, I found them asleep on the floor, face to face, holding one rosary between them, obviously exhausted from several nights of keeping vigil. They had fallen asleep praying for God's help. I could feel the presence of God hovering over them.

I remember being called to anoint a young man who was dying from the complications of AIDS. It was back when AIDS was new on the scene and people were still reacting irrationally. His family, most of his friends and probably his insurance company had abandoned him, with the exception of one compassionate neighbor. The apartment was almost empty, except for a mattress on the floor.

When I arrived, he was filled with guilt, self-loathing and irritation at the church. He was both repulsed and attracted by the idea of a priest coming to see him. I talked to him about the Jesus I knew, the Jesus who welcomed, touched and ate with the marginalized.

At some point, I put my prayer book down and spoke from the heart. As I tried to comfort him with the "good news" that God loves all of us without condition — no ands, ifs or buts about it — I had a strong sense of Jesus speaking through me at that moment.

There are "thin places" everywhere, places where God seems to leak through more easily. Once we have been under one of these "thin places," we do not need "proof" of the existence of God. We understand on some deep level that God's love is shining on us all the time.

October 11, 2007

Looking up, Abraham saw three men standing nearby.
When he saw them, he ran from the entrance
of the tent to greet them.
GENESIS 18

One of the things we should have thought more about before we got into the war in Iraq is the fact that the way people think in the Middle East is not always the way we think in the West. We can't seem to understand that the whole world does not share our values, and when they resist our sharing them, we seem to be shocked.

Our reading today gives us a case in point. If we lived out West in an isolated mountain cabin and we looked up one day to see three men approaching our cabin, we would usher the kids inside and grab our gun. Our first instinct would be to protect ourselves from a threat. If we did not know them, we would no doubt assume, until proven otherwise, that they were up to no good.

If we live in an urban area, we would not think of opening our door to three unknown men who came up on our porch and knocked, especially if we were home alone. We would probably ignore the doorbell, speak to them through a locked screen, make sure we have something handy to protect ourselves or even call the police. If we did not know them, we would no doubt assume, until proven otherwise, that they were up to no good.

In this reading, we see Abraham doing something that we have been warned never to do. In the heat of the day, he is resting in the shade of his tent. When he looks up and sees three men approaching, he runs to meet them, bows down to them, invites them in and treats them like royalty — without even knowing who they are or what they want.

This kind of hospitality is still common among the Middle Eastern nomadic herders of sheep and goats as they try to live much as their ancestors have lived for centuries. Desert nomads, even today, are known for their sumptuous hospitality.

Even in such a situation, biblical hospitality is always a give-and-take proposition. The host knows that strangers always bless them with gifts of their own: news from the outside world, fascinating conversation in a very dull and tedious landscape or maybe a vial of exotic spices from some faraway place. In the case of this reading, Abraham and Sarah hear that they are going to have their first baby even in their advanced age.

I got into writing because of two "angels" appearing unexpectedly in my life: an editor from Crossroads Press and a generous benefactor. Because I was open to their ideas, they keep blessing me.

God undoubtedly has wonderful gifts for you this year. These gifts will very likely be delivered to you by the unlikeliest of people, if you are open to all those who enter your life. This is how God works.

October 18, 2007

Finding Holiness in Your Marriage

Love does not seek its own interests.
1 CORINTHIANS 13:5

During my 37 years of being a priest, I have met many good married people who truly "hunger and thirst for holiness." In more cases than not, they look to become holy by mimicking the spirituality of religious communities, even to the point of becoming associate members.

There is certainly nothing wrong with that, and there is certainly much to be learned from religious communities. But marriage itself is meant to help marriage partners attain holiness in their married life and in welcoming and educating their children.

Obviously, the church needs to do a better job of encouraging marriage partners to look within their own marriages to find their holiness.

In a fascinating passage in the *Catechism of the Catholic Church*, we are told: "There are two sacraments that are directed toward the salvation of others — Matrimony and Holy Orders. If they contribute as well to personal salvation, it is through service to others that they do so."

Just as priests are made holy through serving others as teachers of the Word, ministers of the sacraments and leaders of the community, married people are made holy by becoming good spouses and good parents. Both married couples and priests become holy through their service to others, not by mimicking the spiritualities of others.

The sacrament of marriage gives spouses the grace to mediate the love of Christ to each other, strengthens their indissoluble unity and gives them strength in welcoming and educating children, making them holy in the process.

With Christ dwelling in them, the sacrament of marriage gives married couples the strength they need to endure suffering, to recover after they have fallen, to forgive one another and to bear one another's burdens.

Our culture is forever teaching people that they marry for what it can do for them. As the old Toyota commercial put it, "I love what you do for me." In an old newspaper clipping I have in my "marriage homily file," the woman who held the record on the number of times she had been married put it this way: "All I ever wanted was someone to love me."

The church teaches something quite different. The church teaches us that marriage, one of the sacraments of service, is entered into for the good of others. They marry not so much to be loved as to mediate love to each other, to their children and to the community at large. Maybe the poor woman cited above would have had better luck if she had married to be a benefit to her partner?

With all this said, maybe the best way for marriage partners to become holy is not to "act religious" or "wear their piety on their sleeves," but to devote themselves to being the best spouses and parents they can be, by focusing on being the best people they can be and on what they have to offer their partners and children.

October 25, 2007

See how his lot is with the saints.
WISDOM 5:5

Today we celebrated the Feast of All Saints, a day to honor the memory of the innumerable and nameless men and women who have been welcomed into the kingdom of God. It is one of my favorite feasts.

We tend to think of "saints" as dead people who did great things for God. We tend to think of them as superhuman personalities, people we've put on pedestals to admire.

In New Testament times, believers sometimes called each other "saints." They tended to think of "saints" as living people through whom God was doing great things. For them, being a "saint" was not a status to be earned but a dignity already bestowed as a child of God.

I know some of these "saints" myself, people through whom God has blessed my life and the lives of others in so many ways. They are certainly not your "pious types." They are just ordinary people with extraordinary goodness.

The first one was a single mother of two who was determined to survive her divorce from an abusive husband. She was looking for a parish, people and priests who would not condemn her but encourage her. She did not ask for financial help, but for spiritual and emotional help. She found what she was looking for at the Cathedral of the Assumption.

Even today, with her children raised, she is one of the most positive, most spiritual, most generous women I have ever met. She is pure of heart, with a deep compassion for "underdogs" of all sorts.

The second one is my best friend. He has taught me more about bravery in face of adversity than any bishop, priest or nun. Watching him handle one emotional blow after another, with extraordinary patience, is something I can only hope I would have had if I had been in his shoes. He has a lot to teach about maintaining one's dignity when it is under attack.

The third is a married man, of the handyman variety. He is one of the most avid spiritual seekers I know, even though you would never guess it from the burliness of his looks. He says that he is an agnostic, but I don't believe it. Coming out of a traumatic childhood that would rival one of those unbelievable, horrible exposés on childhood neglect that we see on TV, he has landed on his feet. Self-reflective, he is ravenous in his search to understand the inner workings of himself and others.

The fourth is a retired African-American man who has stayed in touch from my Cathedral days. He is truly a gentle man. Like the widow in the temple, this man gives from his want. Like the woman who anointed the feet of Jesus, he is lavish with his compliments and affirmations. He loves to see people succeed. Humble to the core, he is one of God's anawim.

Like this feast of all saints, today's saints are too many to count.

November 1, 2007

The Spirit is given to each individual for some benefit.
1 CORINTHIANS 12

I have been mistaken for a "charismatic" twice in my life — once in Monticello and once at the Cathedral. Both times I had just delivered a pretty spirited homily for a Roman Catholic priest.

After Mass, both times, a grinning, overly excited woman met me at the door and grabbed me around the shoulders, hugging me tight and squealing, "Oh, Father, I just knew you were one too!"

My eyes bugged out in astonishment. My mind raced to understand her words, "I just knew you were one too?" I thought to myself, "Does she think I am a mental case too? Maybe she thinks I am a drug addict or maybe a confused tourist? Does she know too much? Am going to have to call a lawyer or what?"

Seeing the total confusion and evident fear on my face, she squealed even louder, "A Charismatic, Father, a Charismatic!" Relieved a little and not wanting to let her down too hard, I admitted that I was indeed a charismatic, but only with a very small "c."

Even though I am personally more comfortable with a less emotional and energetic prayer style, I can appreciate the role of the Charismatic Movement in our church. It has mellowed a bit since it first came on the scene a few years back, but it did signal a serious reaction to the overly dull and boring prayer experiences that many Catholics were having.

There is, however, a lot of ground between shouting and snoring, and that ground is where most people I know seem to be comfortable praying. If some people want to shout and pray in tongues, that's fine with me as long as I can still have my quieter style! "There are many gifts, but the same spirit."

As the early church grew, we are told that the disciples did everything they did "by the power of the Holy Spirit." The word "power" in the original Greek is *dunamis* — from which we get our word dynamite.

At our baptisms and confirmations, you and I were given a share of this dynamite, this power of the Holy Spirit, to perform mighty deeds in the world around us. You may not know that you have it, you may not have consciously used it, but you have it inside you —this power of the Holy Spirit for doing great things.

Many times I hear people say they feel powerless. They may feel powerless, but they are not. They may not have owned and tapped into the power of God already within them. We are not powerless. God's power is built into us, waiting to be used for some good purpose. People who believe they are powerless may just be letting themselves off the hook. It takes courage to get up and plug our lives into the power source already within us.

November 8, 2007

*Lord, do you want us to call down
fire from heaven to burn them up?*
LUKE 9:54

These days it seems that everybody is angry, fed-up and aggrieved about something. Here are a few of the things I have heard recently.

"Our dumb president just keeps shooting himself, and us, in the foot!" "The priest in our parish is an idiot!" "Those stupid people who live next door have no regard for anybody else's rights!" "I would love to fry the electrical systems in those cars with the loud music coming from every rolled-down window!" "I want to take her cell phone and shove it down her throat!"

Being angry, fed-up and aggrieved, and being tempted to act on it, is not new. Even some of the great heroes of the Bible were not spared from such feelings and temptations.

In the passage cited above, Jesus and his disciples were cutting through Samaritan territory on their way to Jerusalem. Samaritans hated Jews, and so some Samaritans would not allow them to pass through their town. The angry disciples suggested to Jesus that it might be a good idea call down a ball of fire to fry them, right then and there!

In the Second Book of Samuel, King David was traveling one day when a man named Shimei started cursing him and throwing rocks at him from the side of the road. Abishai, traveling with him, asked David, "Why should this dead dog curse my lord the king? Let me go over and lop off his head."

Today, unfortunately, some people act on their feelings of being angry, fed-up and aggrieved. Every year we see yet another teenager or two taking guns to school to kill those who have tormented or humiliated them. Every day, in some cities, we hear about gang members avenging some personal slight or some encroachment on their territory.

Others turn to the courts. Afternoon television is filled with litigants attempting to get justice from Judge Judy or Judge Joe Brown. Children sue their own parents for a few dollars. Renters sue their tenants over a broken window. Clients sue beauty shop owners for a bad dye or weave job. Dumped lovers sue their former partners for cell phone bills or for the return of an old couch. All this is paid for, of course, by a slew of "ambulance-chasing lawyer" ads.

Still others turn to Jerry Springer for a platform to "slug it out" in front of a national audience over infidelities with each other's relatives. They pull hair, rip clothes and belittle each other with obscenities, to the immense pleasure of a shrieking crowd.

In a world where more people are practicing "an eye for an eye and a tooth for a tooth," it looks as if we are all going to end up blind and toothless. I don't know how to stop it, but I do think there might be some money to be made by investing in seeing-eye dogs and dental clinics.

November 15, 2007

With joy and gratitude for abundance of every kind.
DEUTERONOMY 28:47

This week we celebrate Thanksgiving Day. Giving thanks is a natural response to feelings of gratitude. In other words, we have to feel grateful before we can give thanks. People who feel no gratitude see no need to give thanks.

The feelings of gratitude and the giving of thanks should not be confined, of course, to one day a year. People as blessed as we are should have feelings of gratitude and be moved to give thanks each and every day.

It seems of late that I have often been overcome with gratitude. Gratitude for the big things, yes, but more and more often I'm feeling gratitude for the little things.

For a comfortable relationship with God, a deep love for our church in spite of our weaknesses, a decent prayer life, a sense that my ministry has indeed helped many, for a passion for priesthood that has not waned, for the freedom to do creative ministry, for the ability to be comfortable among the very poor and the very rich.

For a burning desire to improve myself, the ability to forgive and forget, for the courage to stick my neck out, for the ability to accept myself as I am, for having no unfinished business with my dead parents.

For long hours of silence, for the ability to laugh often and be outrageous once in a while, for the resources and the desire to be generous, for a broad range of experiences:

From milking a cow and loading hogs to backpacking in Europe and lecturing before hundreds of priests around the country.

For brothers and sisters, nieces and nephews, for the chance to connect to old friends and new, for a heart that beats and a body that works, for health care and the ability to afford it, for small town roots and city living.

For running water, clean and fresh, hot and cold, at my finger-tips, as much as I need, anytime I want it; for rain, toilets, fishing lakes, swimming pools, steam irons and fire hydrants. For light, heat and air-conditioning.

For food, aisles and aisles of it, homegrown and imported; for strawberries in winter and grapes in the spring; for convenient stores and fast-food restaurants, open all day and all night.

For a place to call home; for a full night's sleep in a clean, comfortable bed; for the private rooms of an outfitted house; for safe neighborhoods; for coats and shoes and clothes for all occasions; for feelings of having enough.

For maps, recipes and directions of all kinds. For counselors and spiritual directors; for hospitals, doctors, police and firemen; for television, telephones and computers; for artists of all types; for comfortable cars, nice roads, airplanes and for the freedom to travel anywhere.

For the regular feelings of gratitude and the good sense to give thanks to the one who keeps on blessing me. For these things, spiritual and material, I am more than thankful.

November 22, 2007

Are We Merely "Dabbling" in Our Faith?

*Anyone who does not hate his parents, spouse,
children and even himself, and does not renounce all
his possessions, cannot be my disciple.*
LUKE 14

My mother had a couple of expressions she would pull out when we were halfhearted and sloppy about our chores around the house: "Your heart's not in it," and "You're just going through the motions."

Sister Rosalinda, our third- and fourth-grade teacher, had her own expression for "halfhearted commitment" as well. One day, one of my old girlfriends was told to clean the blackboard for talking during class. (To protect the guilty, let's call her "Mary.") As she halfheartedly wiped at the board with a rag, Sister Rosalinda took notice and startled all of us with an emphatic yell.

"Mary! Use some elbow grease!" As sister returned to focusing on our class, a very confused Mary went over to the supply cabinet and started rummaging. Seeing this, sister blurted out, "Mary! What are you doing over there? I told you to clean the blackboard." Poor Mary, looking helpless, whimpered back, "Sister, I can't find the elbow grease."

The Gospel cited above is talking about wholehearted commitment to discipleship. We need not get hung up on a literal reading of "hating" your parents, spouse, children, siblings and yourself or renouncing "all" your possessions. This dramatic language is similar to a coach's use of the phrase "giving 110 percent" in sports.

It is a form of exaggeration for emphasis. What Jesus is saying in these powerful phrases is that following him can never be a matter of simply dabbling in religion. He says that we who follow him must give it all we've got. "Our hearts have to be in it." We can't just "go through the motions." We have to "use some elbow grease." We have to "give 110 percent."

Christianity in our time appears to have become a cut-flower religion populated by dabblers. Those, as well, who are willing to settle for tedious expressions of ostentatious piety, micro-managing control tactics and gnat-straining legalisms appear to have hijacked Christianity. These brands of Christianity do not have the ability to inspire people to true greatness.

For this reason, people today do not even attack the church as much as yawn at it. For many, the church has become a yapping, toothless guard dog that many find hard to take seriously. The church is in trouble, not for demanding too much but for demanding too much of the wrong stuff — peripheral stuff, inconsequential stuff. The church needs to ask for nothing less than our whole hearts, our whole minds and whole souls. We need serious commitment without the fanaticism of force.

Christians who claim the name must be able to walk the talk. Some Muslims may hate us, not so much because we are Christians, but because we are not Christian. Gandhi once said in a similar vein, "I like your Christ; I do not like your Christians. Your Christians are so unlike your Christ."

November 29, 2007

Remember the former things, those long ago.
ISAIAH 46: 8

Many readers of this column remember the popular TV show "Cheers." It was set in a Boston bar, owned by a former baseball star, Sam Malone, waitressed by Diane and Carla and frequented by "regulars," Norm, Cliff, Woody and Dr. Frasier Crane. It was a place where people talked about their problems, laughed at each other's flaws and tried to be there when someone needed them.

The "Cheers" theme song goes, "Making your way through the world today takes everything you've got; taking a break from all your worries sure would help a lot. Wouldn't you like to get away? Be glad there is a place in the world where everybody knows your name, and they're always glad you came."

For me, one of those special places "where everybody knows your name and (is) always glad you came" is my old parish of Holy Name of Mary in Calvary, just south of Lebanon, Ky.

In November, I decided to make a surprise visit on the occasion of their annual "turkey supper." What I saw there was a perfect example of how small rural parishes work together flawlessly. They do it, as well, down in St. Theresa Church, my own home parish.

Though I served only three and a half years and left there almost 25 years ago, "everybody knows my name and are always glad I came." The women squealed with delight and smothered me with kisses. The men grabbed me around the shoulders and gave me "bear hugs." It was hard to eat my turkey with all that going on. Every former pastor should be so lucky.

The people of Calvary, like the people of many other small country parishes in our diocese, are among those extraordinary ordinary Catholics who are struggling to keep their parishes going without a resident pastor. They worry about the parish's future and the gradual loss of the young, but for now they are heroically keeping these small faith communities going throughout our diocese. I want to offer all of them an "encouraging word" today. Louisville needs to know you are there.

We recalled our many successful projects, such as the big cleanup day when we corrected years of neglect in one day: two cemeteries, a wooded lot and the grounds around the church property. We retold what seemed like hundreds of funny incidents and Carl Bradshaw stories.

Of course, we brought up that famous farewell dinner, awards show and dance that I arranged as my farewell gift to the parish. Seventy "Knotthead Awards," little plastic trophies with my face on them, were given out that night for anything from "sleeping during Mass" to "the best farfetched story." Some of the people still prize their little trophies.

One of the best phrases to summarize my feelings about that place came out of the mouth of Randall Luckett when he was testifying about something in Frankfort: "I feel sorry for anyone who was not born in Calvary."

December 6, 2007

A dead man was being carried out,
the only son of a widowed mother.
When Jesus saw her, he was moved with pity for her.
LUKE 7

Jesus didn't actually know this poor widow woman, but when he saw her staggering in grief behind her only son's funeral procession, he was overcome with emotion. He wasn't just touched by this pitiful scene — the word used here for "pity" is the strongest word in the Greek language for this emotion, meaning to be moved from the depth of one's being, literally, from one's bowels.

It is the same word used when Jesus encounters a leper kneeling before him, begging for help. The word is used when Jesus encounters the crowds of desperately hungry people on the mountain near the Sea of Galilee. The word is used when Jesus encounters two blind men sitting beside the road on the outskirts of Jericho. It doesn't just mean to feel sorry for. It means to feel to the point of suffering with those who suffer.

Jesus was certainly able to see the loss this woman was experiencing, but he could also see the suffering this poor woman would have to go through for the rest of her life as a sonless widow. Women had no financial security back then. For the rest of her life she was destined to be a charity case for her relatives and friends.

Jesus was certainly able to see the horrific physical ravages that the poor leper was experiencing that day, but he could also see the social, familial and religious isolation that he was enduring because of his disease. Jesus was certainly able to see the physical hunger of the crowds, but he was also able to see their spiritual hunger as well.

Jesus was certainly able to see how difficult the lives of these two men had become because of their blindness, but he could also see how dismissed and marginalized they were by the people around them.

One of the saddest things to happen to those of us called to ministry is to get to the day when we quit caring and quit feeling. We go about our ministry like the priest in the Good Samaritan story, becoming so focused on our "temple duties" that we simply "pass by" bruised and battered people as if they were not there, or we go about our ministry without noticing those who suffer at our gates — like the Dives failed to notice Lazarus.

If I have learned anything from 37 years of priesthood it is this: (1) People will forgive us for just about anything, but not for being cruel, heartless and uncaring, and (2) People will follow us anywhere if we have the ability to touch them, to move them emotionally from our own experience.

As Richard Sklba, Auxiliary Bishop of Milwaukee, put it, "People can be deeply hurt for life by a casual flippant remark or inspired forever by a simple, genuine gesture of kindness."

December 13, 2007

THE BLESSINGS OF A SIMPLIFIED CHRISTMAS

She laid him in a manger.
LUKE 2

I deliberately set out a few years ago to celebrate Christmas differently. For years now, instead of joining in the great frenzy that leads up to Christmas, I work hard during November so that I will have very little to do in December. I don't clear the calendar off so that I can fill it up. I clear it off so that it can stay as empty as possible.

Each year my celebration of Christmas gets simpler and simpler. It started with my brothers and sisters deciding not to exchange gifts. Instead of eating and drinking like there is no tomorrow, I like to keep my eating and drinking simple but good.

Instead of running from one party, engagement or reception to another, I try to make space for big blocks of relaxing time at home. Instead of buying gifts for people I do know, I do random acts of generosity for people I don't know. When it's over, I really feel that I have celebrated Christmas, not just the holidays.

The message of Christmas gets snowed under these days, but it's still there waiting to be uncovered. The message is simple: Out of love for us, Jesus came to be one of us, even one of the most humble among us. It says that after his birth, he was laid in a manager. It doesn't get any simpler than that.

Surely the message Jesus wanted to send was that God wanted to be with us in the simple moments, places and times of our lives. If we experience God this Christmas, it will be because we experienced him in those moments, places and times throughout the last year, not because we went "all out for Christmas."

One of those moments, places and times where I experienced the presence of God this year was at the St. Michael Church men's retreat in November. I led about 35 men, a wonderful balance of young fathers, old fathers and three or four singles, in two days of refection on several areas in their lives, especially looking at their vocations as husbands and fathers in a fresh, new way. We talked about how focusing on being good spouses and parents is how they will ultimately be made holy, as well as how being single gives some of them the freedom to be available to many people.

Being with those young fathers, old fathers and single fathers during those days did as much for me as I was able to do for them. Their responses were very affirming across the board, but one of them gave me a wonderful Christmas present when he ended his note, "You are a credit to your profession."

As a priest, I am called from the laity, to live among the laity so as to empower the laity. If I empowered them to be better husbands and fathers, then they in turn have surely empowered me to be a better priest.

December 20, 2007

*Will he not provide much more for you,
O you of little faith?*
LUKE 12:28

Every New Year's Eve, I have resolved in various forms to "enjoy life more." If the truth were known, however, all the good things of the past several years did not come about because I "resolved" them into existence, but because I was open to receive them as gifts from God.

This is especially true of my ministry at Bellarmine University, Saint Meinrad Seminary and the writing I do for *The Record* each week. All three jobs have certainly helped me "enjoy life more," because all three of them came to me as gifts.

A great deal of my passion during 2008 will most probably be channeled into my work at Saint Meinrad — teaching young priests and priests-to-be as much as I can about "spiritual leadership." I define spiritual leadership as the ability to influence another through invitation, persuasion, example and the skillful use of the church's religious forms to move from where they are to where God wants them to be.

I gathered my ideas on this subject and published them in a book entitled *The Spiritual Leadership of a Parish Priest: On Being Good and Good at It,* which I will use in the class I will be teaching again this semester for those about to be ordained to the priesthood this spring. The class is called "The Transition into Pastoral Ministry."

This class is important because the quality of priestly leadership, in the face of deteriorating religious practice, may be one of Catholicism's most pressing problems.

Teaching this class involves facing several challenges. First, seminaries have traditionally been very strong in teaching seminarians about personal holiness, but not so strong in teaching spiritual leadership or how to lead others to holiness. Priesthood is not just for the benefit of the priest, but even more so for the benefit of the laity. Priests need to be good, but they must also be good at leading others to holiness.

Second, organized religion has lost its power to impose unquestioned rules on the behavior of its members. Instead of blaming themselves for a lack of skills in persuasion and dynamic structures for evangelization, many priests and bishops blame the laity for their lack of faith and the culture for its "secularism" and "moral relativism."

What I am trying to do is to help the clergy of the future to own the fact that the real problem might be their own style and inability to influence others. The solution is not to blame the laity, but to become more skilled in spiritual leadership.

My New Year's resolution this year will be to "have more faith," because I have come to see that the more open I am to God, the better things become for me. This is especially true in the work I have been given to do. As Alan Watts would say, "Faith is, above all, openness; an act of trust in the unknown."

January 10, 2008

*There was a rich man covered with purple and fine linen
who dined sumptuously every day. Lying at his gate was a
poor man covered with sores who longed for
the rich man's table scraps.*
LUKE 16.

"Doing nothing" can actually be illegal. Many countries, but not the United States, have "Good Samaritan Laws" that legally require citizens to assist injured people and people in distress.

Failure to offer assistance in France can be punished by up to five years in prison or 100,000 Euros. This is actually what happened in the case of the photographers who were at the scene of Princess Diana's fatal car accident. They were investigated for violation of the French Good Samaritan Law for their failure to offer assistance.

"Doing nothing" can be sinful as well. This is actually the case in today's beautiful Gospel story about a very rich man and a very poor man. Before we look at the sin here, a sin of omission, let's look at this wonderful story in detail, because in it are details that are stark and shocking.

The rich man has no name, though he has traditionally been called "Dives," meaning "rich" in Latin. Dives, by today's standards, lived in a gated mansion, ate gourmet food every day and dressed in Armani suits. Lazarus, oozing with open sores, we are told, was lying in front of Dives' mansion. From there, this poor man could see loads of food being carried in and out of the mansion, just inside the gates.

Poor Lazarus did not hope to share in that food; he simply longed for the opportunity to eat from the big baskets of scraps being loaded into the dumpster. Rich people back then wiped their hands not on napkins, but on chunks of bread, which were simply thrown away. Because he was too weak from hunger to fight them off, alley dogs came and licked Lazarus' open sores.

Yes, Dives was filthy rich, but that was not his sin. Dives' sin was not that he ordered his security guards to have Lazarus removed from the front of his house. Dives did not even verbally or physically abuse poor Lazarus. There is no indication whatsoever that Dives was evil. He didn't do anything harmful to Lazarus. But that seems to be the point of the whole parable: the rich man did nothing wrong; he simply did nothing.

Let me be clear on one thing. This Gospel is not condemning wealth, but people who are self-absorbed, people who will not look beyond the ends of their own noses. We don't have to be rich to be self-absorbed and blind to the suffering of those around us. The sin here is not wealth, because "to whom much is given, much is expected."

The first step to helping those around us who suffer is noticing them. The second step is to realize that true Christianity is not just about avoiding evil. Failure to do good things is often just as sinful as doing bad things.

January 17, 2008

Prayer of this kind is good.
1 TIMOTHY 2:3

Most of us who believe in the practice of prayer find it hard these days to find time to pray. Sadly, this is true of many priests as well. Since we cannot create more hours in a day, we have to be clever and imaginative with the hours we have.

My favorite place to pray privately has become my car. It is one of the few places left where I am not interrupted or distracted. Since I drive back and forth from Louisville to Saint Meinrad once or twice a week, I have more time to pray than I first thought.

When I started working at Saint Meinrad a little more than three years ago, I would never think of leaving home without a stack of CDs or tapes or turning on the radio to fill the time in my car. For more than a year now, I have made the trip in total silence. I have grown to love it and look forward to it. In this silence, my mind seems to naturally turn to prayer. The scenery makes it even more conducive to praying.

On Mondays, to miss the downtown morning rush, I usually get up at 4:30 a.m. and, with coffee in hand, I am on the road by 5:15 a.m. Some mornings I can see a beautiful red sun coming up over the horizon, and on occasion a full moon fills my rear view mirror. In the fall, waves and waves of colorful trees blanket the hills. In the winter those same trees, gray and bare, stand quietly in new snow. In the spring, redbuds and dogwoods precede the contagious darkening of green leaves.

Part of the trip takes me through the Hoosier National Forest. From childhood, I have known that "the woods" is a place of wonderment, a sacred space. A little bit of that sacredness seeps into me, even if I am only driving through it.

Racing cars and roaring trucks pass me easily even when I am pushing the speed limit myself. They are made frantic by some unknown pressure, and I pray for their peace of mind.

Laborers in pickups and mothers in minivans all get prayed for as I drive along in silence.

I pass farms where I am reminded, up close and personal, to be grateful for my daily bread — where it comes from and what it takes to get it to me. I pray for these and indeed all farmers.

I usually arrive as thunderous bells gather the monks for their 5:30 a.m. prayer time. As I walk into the huge complex, it is not lost on me that I work at a place saturated with 150 years of such praying.

This is my prayer time. I recommend that you find your prayer time, your special time/place where you can sit in the presence of God in gratitude and bless the people in the world around you.

January 24, 2008

Be transformed by the renewal of your mind.
ROMANS 12:2

One of the most interesting things that happened to me over Christmas was an experience I had standing in the cash register line at a Walgreens drugstore. It occurred right before Christmas. It wasn't what happened in front of me that was so interesting, but what happened within me.

A smallish young woman, holding a beautiful, blanket-wrapped baby boy, was digging through her purse with one hand to find enough change to pay for what was on the counter. She was taking so long that I could feel myself becoming more and more irritated the longer it took.

All of a sudden, I made the decision to look at what was happening in another way. I chose to view the situation from her perspective instead of mine. She was obviously growing more embarrassed and frustrated as she dug with one hand and then the other, shifting her baby from one arm to the other. I finally blurted out, "How much do you need? $2? I've got it! Have a Merry Christmas!"

Relieved, she thanked me profusely and then stepped forward to give me a hug. The people in line and the cashier were obviously moved by what they had witnessed. As I got into my truck, I realized that scenario would have been a completely different experience if I had not changed my mind and had not chosen to react differently to what was happening in front of me.

Maybe you have been angry with an old spouse, an adult child or a parent for a very long time. It is an unhealed sore on your consciousness. You can't quit remembering it, and so you continue to be hurt by it. You can change all that by simply changing your mind. You can choose to forgive and let it go, not so much to let them off the hook, but to let yourself off the hook.

Maybe you have been "getting little out of church" for a long time. You can change all that by simply changing your mind. Instead of expecting somebody else to make it meaningful for you, you can start doing some things on your own that will make it meaningful for you.

When we change our minds, we create a different world for ourselves. With a changed mind, we can experience old realities in a new way. This is what Jesus really wants from us this Lent, not tedious little mind games with candy bars.

Metanoiete! Change the way you look at things. Change the way you think. With this word, we open the season of Lent next Wednesday. Our goal is to the reach Easter with open eyes, eyes that can see the work of God going on all around us, even if it is as small as a mustard seed and as quiet as yeast. As St. Paul wrote to the Roman Christians, "Be transformed by the renewal of your mind."

January 31, 2008

*He shall strike the ruthless with the rod of his mouth;
with the breath of his lips he shall slay the wicked.*
ISAIAH 11:4

John the Baptizer has to be one of the hardest persons in the whole Bible to warm up to. He is the kind of man who would make you would grab the kids and pull them close if you ran into him on the streets.

The smell coming from him alone would probably gag a horse. He made his home in caves out in the desert wilderness. He wore a disgusting camel hide and ate locusts, wild honey and probably anything else he could find crawling on the sand.

This hairy, bellowing preacher-man did not mince words. He tore into religious leaders, calling them "nests of poisonous snakes." He did not stop there.

John took on the political establishment as well. On one occasion, he got up in King Herod's face and publicly confronted him with the fact that he was committing adultery with his brother's wife. For that tacky little speech, Herod had John's head severed and served up on a platter.

John was a "prophet," and this kind of radical truth-telling is what prophets do. Prophets are not so much people who predict the future as they are people who rub the truth of the present in our faces and make us look at it.

We might call such people today "whistle-blowers," people who drag the truth out into the light of day and make us look at it, whether it is convenient to look or not. Like prophets of old, whistle-blowers are often considered "nut cases" at first. Like prophets of old, whistle-blowers often get themselves killed, either actually or figuratively, because most establishments do not like to have their boats rocked or their truths aired. Instead of heeding the message, they usually turn on the messenger.

If you have ever been involved in exposing one of these inconvenient truths, you know just how dangerous it can be. If you are not physically hurt, you can be labeled or blackballed for years or maybe for life.

We still kill our prophets in a host of creative ways. We shun friends who will not go along with us when we do wrong. We ridicule the teaching of the church, especially when it won't bless the wrong we want to do. Prophets won't let us get away with that, and so they are hated.

All of us have "built-in prophets" as well. Our built-in prophets are called "consciences." Our consciences are constantly confronting us with truths that we would just as soon not acknowledge. We can numb them temporarily with alcohol or even kill them for good with regular and consistent violations.

Maybe the message of John the Baptist is summarized best and most simply by Marcus Aurelius: "If it is not right, do not do it. If it is not true, do not say it."

February 7, 2008

If I do not have love, I am nothing.
1 CORINTHIANS 13:2

Even though the church has dropped St. Valentine from its official list of saints, that will not stop me from saying a few words about love and marriage on this very important Hallmark occasion.

Every time I get up to preach at a wedding, I can imagine people sitting in front of me saying to themselves, "Now what on earth does he know about marriage? He's never been married."

Well, I may not know too much about marriage, but I know at least as much as most of those for whom I have witnessed weddings. I may have not been married before, but let me remind you that neither have they.

Even though marriage and priesthood appear to be polar opposites, in reality they are very similar. The Catechism of the Catholic Church says there are two sacraments directed toward the salvation of others: marriage and priesthood. In other words, people get married not for their own good, but for the good of their partners and their children, while men become priests not for their own good, but for the good of the people they serve.

It goes on to say that what will make a married person holy and lead them to heaven is being a good spouse and parent, while what will make a priest holy and lead him to heaven is being a good spiritual leader for his parishioners.

With that said, let me share with you some practical suggestions to think about in doing the hard work of marriage, something I call the two great "commandments of marriage." They are built on the two great commandments of Jesus, "Love God with all your heart and your neighbor as yourself."

Love God with all your hearts. Married partners do well never to forget who it was who brought them together to begin with. It was God who brought them together, even though he may have used certain people and specific circumstances to do it.

Marriage partners do well to keep God as a partner, asking him to walk hand-in-hand with them over the years, making it their practice to go to church together regularly, adopting the practice of praying together before meals in their home, thanking God in times of joy and success, and leaning on God in times of disappointment and trouble.

Having a close relationship with God makes good practical sense as well. It has been proven statistically, again and again, that marriages with God in them are much happier and last much longer than marriages that don't.

Love your neighbor as yourself. A marriage partner's closest neighbor will be his or her spouse. Love, in marriage, is not just about having warm feelings for each other. It is even more so about doing good deeds for each other, and doing them whether it feels good or not. "Loving your neighbor" has always been more about loving and caring actions than sentimental feelings.

February 14, 2008

THE NEED FOR SPIRITUAL LEADERSHIP

Let the leader be as a servant.
LUKE 22:26

It is not news that we leaders of organized religion have lost our ability to force unquestioned rules on the behavior of our members.

As a priest who has been trying to teach the next generation of priests about spiritual leadership, I have had the opportunity to observe, study and research this needed skill in the church as well as to reflect deeply on my own experience as a spiritual leader. You cannot teach what you do not know.

After piloting a presbyteral assembly model in several dioceses, at which members of the laity were invited to speak, we are learning that what the laity want most from their priests is "spiritual leadership" ability. They want their priests to be holy, yes, but they also want them to be able to lead others to holiness.

Instead of blaming ourselves for our inability to persuade and our inability to inspire, some priests persist in blaming the laity for their lack of faith and the culture for its "secularism" and "moral relativism."

The most obvious sign of our spiritual leadership failure is religion's creeping enmeshment in partisan politics. Instead of turning to politics as a way to make people do what we believe they should do, we need to focus on strengthening our own spiritual leadership abilities. True spiritual leadership, as Pope Benedict XVI has insisted, is about the ability to influence another through invitation, persuasion and example to go where God wants them to go.

Instead of blaming others or trying to force people into conformity, we need to admit that the real problem might be our own styles of evangelization, our inability to inspire and our lack of skill in influencing others.

Seminaries are doing a good job of teaching personal holiness, but we also are trying to do a better job of teaching seminarians to be spiritual leaders and teachers of holiness. The whole purpose of being priests, according to Pope John Paul II, is to help the people of God carry out their ministry.

I recently finished writing a book entitled, *The Spiritual Leadership of a Parish Priest: On Being Good and Good at It.* I had been working on it ever since I realized the need for this emphasis in seminary training. I am happy to say that some of these ideas have made their way into the pastoral curriculum.

If priests are to be effective spiritual leaders, they must claim their pulpits and become masters of ritual. If they want to revive the church, they must build a fire in the pulpit, and if they are going to lead a sacramental church, they must learn how to use the rituals of the church effectively.

Those who would hold positions of authority in the church must avoid two extremes: authoritarianism and abdication. Priests must know their place in the church and embrace it, while respecting the place of others. They are not the only leaders, but they must especially be spiritual leaders.

February 21, 2008

CHARACTER, INTEGRITY, PRINCIPLE AND COURAGE

*We are ready to die rather than transgress
the laws of our ancestors.*
2 MACCABEES

When I was a teenaged seminarian out at the now-closed St. Thomas Seminary on old Brownsboro Road, we used to come into the dining room for lunch in silence, standing at our assigned tables until everybody was assembled, before we sat down together.

Before we started eating, we used to listen to one of the older students read the story of one of the martyrs who had given his life for the faith. Every day we heard about courageous saints who had gotten their heads or hands chopped off, who had been boiled in oil, shot full of arrows, hanged or crucified.

It didn't do too much for one's appetite.

Often, as I sat there listening, I wondered whether I would have the courage to lay down my life for the faith in such a situation or whether I would lie to my torturers' faces in an attempt to save my own life. The priests at the seminary always told us that God would give us the courage we needed at times like that, but I always hoped I would never have to find out.

Today's reading is about character, integrity, principle and courage. It is about a saintly Jewish mother and her seven courageous sons who were forced to choose between

48

their religious principles and expediency. They were forced to choose between what would get them ahead for the moment and what would get them ahead in the long run.

Talk about a story about character, integrity, principle and courage. This woman not only watched all of her children be tortured and killed right before her eyes, she even egged them on before she herself was killed with them. This has to be one of the best hero stories in all of Scripture.

Would you be willing to die for your Catholic faith? Sadly, most of us wouldn't because we do not live in a culture where character, integrity, principle and courage are generally valued. We live in a culture of expediency, the "latest, best offer" and "service on demand."

It is hard to imagine dying for the faith in an age when character, integrity, principle and courage are so rare. Without those qualities, however, heroism is impossible. As long as most of our heroes are drug-addicted TV personalities and overpaid athletes, character, integrity, principle and courage will never be valued. Instead of plastering their pictures in our rooms or hanging on their every word, the following people's words might serve us better:

J.C. Watts of Texas once said, "Character is doing the right thing when nobody's looking. There are too many people who think the only thing that's right is to get by, and the only thing that's wrong is to get caught."

Will Rogers once wrote, "Live in such a way that you would not be ashamed to sell your parrot to the town gossip."

February 28, 2008

"Thank God I am not like the rest of humanity!"
LUKE 18:11

One of the things I like about Luke's Gospel is that the tables are always being turned. Losers win and winners lose. The underdog regularly comes out as the hero. We see it yet again in this Gospel.

Here we are presented with two men praying in the Temple. The man up front is a Pharisee, a holy man, a conscientious keeper of religious laws in their minutest detail. He does everything right, but his religious success has made him proud. He is so proud of his meticulous religious observance that even his prayer has become an exercise in informing God about just how good he is.

He is so arrogant, and so needs to be "better than," that he goes so far as to put down the man praying in the back of the Temple. "Thank God," he prays, "that I am not like everybody else — greedy, dishonest and adulterous— and especially like that tax collector back there."

The Pharisee probably wasn't greedy, dishonest or adulterous, but his success at being good was ruined by his pride and self-righteousness. Instead of praising God in his prayer, he praises himself.

The man in the back was a tax collector, known for squeezing money out of his fellow Jews, even out of the poorest of the poor, for himself and for the hated Roman government. He too was praying, but his prayer was different. He simply beats his breast while looking downward, saying "God, have mercy on me! I am a sinner and I know it!"

The man in the front was good, but proud. The man in the back was bad, but humble. Jesus praises the bad, but humble, man's prayer, and dismisses the good, but proud, man's prayer.

The crowds of ordinary people listening to this little story, people on the edges of religious observance, would have burst into applause at the punch line. They hated pride-filled religious types then as much as we do today.

Even though this Gospel is, on the surface, about prayer, it has something important to teach us about our reactions to some of the human tragedies that go on around us.

It is always easy to stand by self-righteously and say to ourselves, "Thank God I am not like her or him!" Should we not rather beat our breasts and say, "O God, be merciful to me a sinner?"

In no way should we deny the horror of what some people do, but if I have learned anything about myself and other people during 38 years of priesthood it is this: all of us are capable of about anything under the right circumstances. Truly, "there, but for the grace of God, go we."

Today's Pharisees, especially the radio and TV types, still like to brag about how good they are compared to "those other people." Some good old breast beating and mercy seeking might actually serve them, and us, better.

March 6, 2008

We accept good things from God.
Should we not then accept the bad?
JOB 2:10

Why do good people have to suffer through things like the ravages of cancer and its treatments, only to die?

I have been asked various versions of this question, as well as heard versions of attempted answers, throughout my almost 38 years of priesthood. My answer is simple. I haven't the foggiest idea, and neither does anyone else. The bottom line is, nobody really knows, including those of good will who try to come up with something comforting to say.

It is better, I think, to just sit with the mystery. Anything else comes across as irritatingly trite or nauseatingly sentimental.

The biblical story of Job makes this very point. One day, God and the devil discuss the Job family. Even God brags about how good and faithful the Job family has been. The devil listens to all God has to say about them, but then says to God, "Sure! Who wouldn't love you if they had it as good the Job family has it? It's easy to believe when things are going well, but just start taking a few things away from them and then you'll see just how faithful they are."

In this little play, God allows Satan to start taking things away to test Job's fidelity. First, Job loses his money.

Next, he loses his children in a freak accident. Finally, Job loses his health. Through all this, the last line of our reading tells us that Job never curses God, even though his wife suggests it. He neither questions God nor does anything sinful.

The story ends without a convincing reason being given for Job's suffering. However, because Job remained faithful in the absence of answers, God makes the latter part of Job's life even better than the first!

When we are faced with the mystery of suffering and death, we have no real answers. However, we do have a choice about how we want to respond. We can be bitter about what we lost, or we can be grateful for what we had. Entitlement leads us into bitterness. Gratitude leads us into peaceful acceptance. When we feel entitled, gratitude is impossible.

Feelings of entitlement make us believe that life owes us something, and when it is taken away, we feel angry, resentful, cheated and frustrated. However, in reality, entitlement is an illusion. With life being as it is, entitlement is a perfect setup for disappointment because it is based on a lie to begin with. We are owed nothing in this life, and the truth of the matter is, everything is a gift. We deserve nothing, and everything is on loan — even our loved ones.

On the other hand, if we believe that life and everything in it is a gift, we can experience painful losses, even death, in a radically different way. Instead of being bitter about what we lost, we can become grateful for what we had.

March 13, 2008

Keep watch over yourselves and over the flock the
Holy Spirit has given you to guard.
ACTS 20:28

It's Holy Thursday, the day when we traditionally celebrate the institution of the priesthood. Normally, on this occasion I write something about my own experience of priesthood, but this year I want to share with you a "chain letter" that I received through the mail a few months ago. It might say more about your experience than anything else I have read. Maybe you have already seen it.

It said, "A recent survey in America has compiled all the qualities that people expect from the perfect priest. These were fed into a computer and the results showed that the perfect priest was 28 years of age, tall, slim, athletic and handsome.

"He preaches for exactly 10 minutes. He frequently condemns sin and social evils, but never upsets anyone. He works tirelessly from 6:30 a.m. to 11 p.m. and is also a janitor.

"He earns $100 a week, wears good clothes, buys good books, drives a good car and gives about $50 a week to the poor.

"He is a man of limitless patience, gentleness and kindness, but also strong, vigorous and a decisive leader.

"He gives of himself completely to others, but never gets too close to anyone lest he be criticized.

"He has a burning desire to work with teenagers, but spends all his time with senior citizens.

"He spends his entire day in parish visitations, in comforting the sick and bereaved and in working in the schools, but is always in the office when anyone phones or calls.

"He is a man of deep spirituality and wide learning, but of down-to-earth practicality, a capable administrator, a financial genius, a wise counselor, an architect and a builder.

"If your priest does not measure up to these expectations, simply send this letter to six other parishes also tired of their priest. Then bundle up your priest and send him to the church at the top of the list. In one week you will receive 1,643 priests in return, and at least one of these should be perfect.

"Have faith in this letter. One parish broke the chain and got their old priest back in less than three weeks."

With our local priest personnel board meeting around the clock to make ends meet this June, maybe this letter will give you something to think about.

There are 27,000 priests active in parish ministry in the United States today, and there are approximately 60 million Catholics. The number of priests is shrinking, and the number of Catholics is growing. The ratio of priests to parishioners is about 1 to 1,200. The average age of diocesan priests in the United States is 57. Presently, 16 percent of all priests active in parish ministry have come from other countries. The largest national representations in this group are as follows: Ireland, India, the Philippines, Poland, Vietnam, Mexico, Columbia and Nigeria.

Have you hugged your priest today?

March 20, 2008

I will not leave you orphaned.
JOHN 14:18

God has always been portrayed in Scripture as having a soft spot in his heart for the orphan and the widow. Jesus and Mary, who probably lost Joseph when Jesus was young, knew firsthand what it was like to be an orphan and a widow.

It is not surprising, then, that one of the things that Jesus promised his disciples at the Last Supper, who were overcome with fear of being abandoned, was not to leave them orphaned, but to send them the Holy Spirit as a Comforter.

Many people over the years have been "orphaned" in the literal sense of the word, either through abandonment, kidnapping or death. I cannot begin to imagine how traumatic that would be for any child, especially those old enough to know what is going on.

Even more people have been "orphaned" in a figurative sense. They have been divorced by their spouses, left as widows or widowers by untimely deaths, jilted by fiancés or dumped by close friends or "significant others."

Having had no choice in what happened, they are left traumatized. They carry those hollow feelings in the pit of their stomachs. Their hearts ache. Their minds bounce between denial, bargaining and anger. Their obsessive thinking about it nearly drives them crazy as they try to make their way to acceptance. Some never recover from their feelings of being abandoned.

Abandonment issues are very powerful in the lives of many, many people. It's the fear of being alone and fear of not being able to handle what life throws at them. As social beings, created for interconnection, fear of losing those connections runs deep. Genesis tells us that the very first sin ever committed involved a denial of that simple fact.

We are social beings, but what can we do when we have to face a major severing of the connection between ourselves and a loved one? Some people go for years believing that if they just don't like it enough, they will earn a reversal of that fact. When that doesn't happen, they end up carry an oozing sore of bitterness for years and years — sometimes to their graves.

One of the most moving outreaches to these people that I ever heard about are the "Blue Christmas Masses" that are offered by a growing number of parishes during the Christmas holidays when the loss, grief and loneliness of many come into sharp relief.

Prayer is sometimes about the only lifeline many people have during these traumatic times. For some, prayer helps about as much as anything, especially the kind of prayer that asks for a reconciliation with reality. But isn't that the best kind of prayer — the kind that asks God to help us accept his will, instead of asking God to change his will? Mary, the Sorrowful Mother, who herself was left widowed and childless, is a perfect model for those who feel abandoned by those they love.

March 27, 2008

He has gone to stay at a sinner's house.
LUKE 19:1-10

"You can't judge a book by its cover." We have all heard this warning about disappointing contents coming in beautiful packaging. All of us, no doubt, have been fooled into buying a book with an attractive cover or have rented a movie with a great-sounding trailer that turned out to be garbage.

In the religious world, "you can't judge a book by its cover" is true as well. Many, no doubt, have been fooled by "religious types" with their great made-for-TV images who were really nothing more than "wolves in sheep's clothing."

In the spiritual world, "you can't judge a book by its cover" is true as well in a very different sense. The story of Zacchaeus is a case in point. On the outside, he appears to be a rotten, low-life sinner, but he turns out to be a humble, generous and religious man. "You can't judge a book by its cover" in his case either.

Externally, Zacchaeus was a sawed-off, greedy, little crook in the eyes of his hometown folks. He was up to his eyeballs in an extortion racket under the auspices of the hated Roman government. He was one of those tax collectors hired by the occupying Roman authorities to squeeze money out of his fellow Jews, especially the poorest of the poor — money that would line the pockets of the Roman

Emperor and Zacchaeus himself. He appeared to be one rotten, little scumbag.

In the Old Testament we read, "People see externals, but God sees into the heart." Nowhere do we see this more clearly than in a side-by-side comparison of Zacchaeus and those who judged him.

On one hand, the Pharisees appeared to be holy, upstanding members of the community. Underneath, however, they were rotten to the core. Jesus called them "whitewashed tombs that looked good on the outside, but inside were filled with stench and rottenness."

On the other hand, Zacchaeus appeared to be a rotten, no-good, sinner in the eyes of all the people. Jesus, however, because he had the ability to see into hearts, did have the ability to judge a book by its cover.

When he looked up in the tree and saw Zacchaeus, he saw a lot of goodness down deep inside this little man. "People see externals, but God sees into the heart."

Since we can only see people's outsides while God can see into people's hearts, Jesus warned us not to judge each other. We never know for sure what's going on inside people. It's a sound spiritual practice, therefore, to give each other the benefit of the doubt.

I have spent most of my priesthood reaching out to people whose magnificent goodness was hidden under some pretty awful appearances. Some of the meanest Catholics I have ever met have been those "pillar of the church" types, while some of the most devout Catholics have been those who have been rejected or hurt by the church.

April 3, 2008

*The person who is dishonest in very small matters
is also dishonest in great ones.*
LUKE 10

Some of you no doubt remember the 1997 Jim Carey movie, "Liar! Liar!" It is a comedy about a career-focused lawyer and divorced father, Fletcher Reede, who is in the habit of lying about almost everything.

After lying and missing his son's birthday party, the son blows out the candles of his cake and makes a wish. The wish is that his father cannot lie for 24 hours. The films unwinds as Fletcher has several embarrassing instances where he blurts out exactly what he is thinking and figures out that he is unable to lie.

It is a very funny movie, but isn't it odd that the reason it is so funny is that we so often lie to each other that telling the truth all the time is actually funny to us? As Noel Coward put it, "It's discouraging to think how many people are shocked by honesty and how few by deceit."

Integrity is about doing the right thing for the right reason even when nobody is looking.

From something as simple as a lying repairman who says, "I'll be there first thing Monday morning," to a president lying about the Watergate break-in, we are growing used to lying. It is estimated that 28 percent of married men and 18 percent of married women cheat on their marriage partners. Fifty percent of all college students, under pressure, cheat at least once. Coaches in professional sports are "busted" regularly for cheating. As George Orwell put it, "During times of universal deceit, telling the truth becomes a revolutionary act."

The first step in building a life of integrity as a Catholic Christian is to find out what morals and principles are truly Christian and Catholic. We cannot be Catholic Christians without knowing what principles Catholic Christians follow. Once we really know what these principles are, we will discover they are indeed counter-cultural.

The second step in building a life of integrity as a Catholic Christian is to review the choices we have been making in our past and observe how much we have, or have not, lived by those principles. Before we can choose otherwise, we have to own the choices we have been making up til now.

The third step in building a life of integrity as a Catholic Christian is to decide what needs to change to align our behaviors more closely to the principles we profess to follow.

The fourth step in building a life of integrity as a Catholic Christian is to monitor the decisions we make every day, however big or small, and how close they bring us to being the person of integrity we want to be. As Jesus puts it in today's Gospel, if we can't be trusted in very small matters, we can never be trusted in great matters.

Let us be revolutionaries in a time of "universal deceit." Let us strive to be people of flawless integrity.

April 10, 2008

Cast me not off in my old age.
PSALMS 71:9

I will be 64 years old on Monday. No matter how you cut the cake, there are more slices behind me than in front of me.

I would probably not think too much about old age if it weren't for working around so many young people at Saint Meinrad and at Bellarmine University. They may "keep you young," as the old saying goes, but they are always reminding you how old you are as well.

How many times have I spewed my cereal all over people at the breakfast table at the seminary when one of them announces that their "grandfather was 64 today?" They always seem to be moved to add, "I can't believe how old he is," for emphasis, before saying innocently, "Oh, I'm sorry Father!" right before bursting into laughter.

Maybe this is why I have always loved hanging out with old people. They give me a break from all that youthful, age-unconscious energy. At least they think I am young, no matter how old I get.

So far, my life has only gotten better and better with age, and I am counting on 64 being even better than 63. My goal is to be the happiest old priest who is not in "the old priests' home." With a big dose of denial and a whole lot of optimism, I hope to go out with a grin on my face.

Working from the belief that "if you don't laugh, you cry," let me share with you some of the wisdom I have collected on this issue. Since I am not old yet, this wisdom is, of course, meant for those older than I am. "For the first half of your life, people tell you what you should do; for the second half, they tell you what you should have done." (Richard Needham)

"At 20 we worry about what others think of us; at 40 we don't care about what others think of us; at 60 we discover they haven't been thinking about us at all." (Malcolm Forbes)

"The first half of life consists of the capacity to enjoy without the chance; the last half consists of the chance without the capacity." (Mark Twain)

"One can remain alive long past the usual date of disintegration if one is unafraid of change, insatiable in intellectual curiosity, interested in big things, and happy in a small way." (Edith Wharton)

"Wisdom doesn't necessarily come with age. Sometimes age just shows up all by itself." (Tom Wilson)

"Old age is like flying through a storm. Once you're aboard, there's nothing you can do." (Golda Meir)

"Youth is a gift of nature, but age is a work of art." (Garson Kanin)

"The older the fiddle, the sweeter the tune." (English Proverb)

"First you forget names, then you forget faces. Next you forget to pull your zipper up and finally, you forget to pull it down." (George Burns)

Happy Birthday, one and all, whenever it is.

April 17, 2008

There's No Doubt Laughter Is Good Medicine

The one enthroned in heaven laughs.
PSALM 2:4

Maybe it helps assure me that I am not the craziest person in the world, but I keep a running tab of curious stories from the news. Some are sad. Some are funny. Some are merely bizarre.

The History Channel let me know recently that more than a million Americans worship Satan. Why am I not surprised?

Christmas before last, the TV show "Fear Factor" featured participants who were encouraged to eat some of the most disgusting things imaginable. Nothing new, but this time the disgusting "edibles" were wrapped and placed under a tree. As each contestant opened his or her package, they were wished "Merry Christmas." What happened to a lump of coal or a bundle of switches?

One commercial for grape juice shows a scared little kid, afraid of monsters, trying to go to sleep. When his father comes into his room to comfort him, the little boy says, "Don't worry, daddy, the antioxidants (in the grape juice) will protect me." Whatever happened to God and the angels?

Maybe it was year before last, but a new movie premiered on Christmas Day. It was called "Darkness." What about Isaiah, who said, "The people have seen a great light?"

A Hollywood wedding recently featured dogs in tuxedos carrying the wedding rings down the aisle. Another reason why priests, ministers and rabbis universally dread weddings these days.

Sadly, but ironically, one of America's top, young chefs is battling tongue cancer. I was reminded of Euell Gibbons, the famous health nut who used to recommend that people eat pine cones and who died of a bleeding ulcer.

An 88-year-old man died last year, but right before dying, he dropped 34 humorous Christmas cards in the mail to his friends with a return address "heaven." He sort of reminds me of a famous tombstone with these words engraved on it: "I told you I was sick."

One of the funniest compliments I received last year was one I overheard from my niece's young son. After loading their car with some good stuff that I needed to get rid of and giving him and his sisters a few bucks for spending money, he asked his mother, "What is he, a modern-day Mother Teresa?"

As I write this, I was reminded of my job at the seminary. I probably have laughed more there over the last three years than anywhere else since I left it 38 years ago. Many people think that seminaries are overly serious places, when in fact they are places where laughter regularly resonates up and down the dining room and hallways.

A Yiddish proverb says, "What soap is to the body, laughter is to the soul." Voltaire says, "God is a comedian, playing to an audience too afraid to laugh."

As we go through life, with its sad, curious and bizarre moments, it may be good sometime to stop and laugh at the insanity, because "if you don't laugh, you cry."

April 24, 2008

The Poetic Language About the Virgin Mary

Hail favored one! Most blessed are you among women.
LUKE 1:28,42

May is the month in which we celebrate Mary in a very special way.

All of us who were blessed (and I, for one, certainly do mean "blessed") with a Catholic school education in years past can readily recall tender memories of the annual "May processions." They always culminated in the crowning of a statue of the Blessed Virgin Mary.

As I reflected on the Feast of the Immaculate Conception last December, I was reminded of something my grandfather always said and several things that I have learned or observed over the years.

My grandfather had an expression that has stuck with me. He used to say, "Nobody puts a $50 saddle on a $5 horse." By that he meant that people in their right minds should never invest something of value in something that is worthless to begin with.

As a person who has remodeled several houses, that feast also reminded me of some of the things I have learned in the process. I have learned that it is never a good idea to waste good money trying to remodel a house that was poorly built.

Even a complete idiot at dating knows that if you want to give your fiancée a gorgeous, expensive diamond for an engagement present, you should never think of having such a diamond set in a cheap plastic ring. A gorgeous diamond should be put it in a worthy ring — a ring with enough gold to hold it securely and to show it off.

There is a lot of poetic language surrounding the feasts of Mary — virgin mother and sinless woman, to name two of the most common. What those words are saying is simple. When God decided to become one of us, to come to us in the flesh of a human being, he chose the right "setting" for this precious gift, a gift infinitely more precious than the Hope Diamond could ever be. He chose Mary, the favored one, blessed among all women, sinless from birth, as the mother of Jesus and Mother of God.

Just as no one would put a $50 saddle on a $5 horse, waste good money remodeling a falling-down wreck of a house or place a precious diamond in a cheap plastic ring, God chose Mary as a worthy setting for his most precious gift to humankind — his only son. In a nutshell, this is the message behind all the poetic language we are given for our ancient Marian feasts.

Devotion to Mary has suffered over the years in two ways. First, overly pious and sentimental exaggerations in favor of such devotion have been off-putting except to the most simple of faith. Second, strictly logical arguments have been off-putting except to the most rigidly rationalistic.

Poetry is the language of love and logic the language of science, but both communicate their own kind of truth.

May 1, 2008

What is Truth?
JOHN 19:38

There's a whole lot of untruth being perpetuated in our world. From advertising to the Internet, "there's a sucker born every minute." People today crave truth so much that they are highly susceptible to any "truth oil salesman" on the block.

George Orwell once said, "In a time of universal deceit, telling the truth is a revolutionary act."

"When a well-packaged web of lies has been sold gradually to the masses over generations, the truth will seem utterly preposterous and its speaker a raving lunatic." (Dresden James)

"I believe that unarmed truth and unconditional love will have the final word in reality. This is why right, temporarily defeated, is stronger than evil triumphant." (Martin Luther King Jr.)

"Sometimes the majority only means that all the fools are on the same side." (Unknown)

We have all heard the saying that the truth hurts. "The truth will set you free, but first it will make you miserable." (President James A. Garfield)

"The truth is 'hate speech' only to those who have something to hide." (Michael Rivero)

Not all of those who profess to know the truth actually do. "The truth is rarely pure and never simple." (Oscar Wilde)

"Nothing in all the world is more dangerous than sincere ignorance and conscious stupidity." (Martin Luther King Jr.) 57

"Believe those who are seeking the truth; doubt those who find it." (Andre Gide)

"The enemy of the truth is very often not the lie — deliberate, contrived and dishonest, but the myth — persistent, persuasive and unrealistic." (John F. Kennedy)

Simply professing the truth will not necessarily make a person virtuous. "One truth out of context can prove very dangerous." (Gregory Phillips) "The truth is often a terrible weapon of aggression. It is possible to lie, and even murder, with the truth." (Alfred Adler)

Sometimes people try to make true what they love, instead of loving the truth. "A thing is not necessarily true because a man dies for it." (Oscar Wilde) "Intense feeling too often obscures the truth." (Harry S. Truman) "My mind is made up. Don't confuse me with the facts." (an old saying)

"If a thousand old beliefs were ruined in our march to truth we must still march on." (Tom Waits) "From the cowardice that shrinks from new truth; from laziness that is content with half-truths; from the arrogance that thinks it knows all truth — O God of Truth deliver us!" (Unknown)

We must start somewhere to "know" truth. We either start with man being the one who can determine what truth is, or we start with God being the only one who can determine what truth is. The truth either is or is not. Truth does not need to be accepted, felt or voted on to be true.

God's truth is revealed in Scripture. The Holy Spirit leads the church in understanding and teaching the fullness of truth found in Scripture. For more information, "Google" Pope John Paul II's "*Veritatis Splendor*."

May 8, 2008

LIFE IS ABOUT "CREATING YOURSELF"

Thirty-eight down and an unknown number to go. Tomorrow I will celebrate my 38th anniversary of ordination and begin the 39th year of priesthood. My, how the time flies when you're having fun!

My worst nightmare has not been the work I have had to do as a priest, but the fear that I might lose interest in it. I can say that priesthood has gotten better and better, and my passion for priesthood has actually grown over the last 38 years. I cannot imagine being bored with priesthood or being dead on my feet doing it.

Between my work at Bellarmine University and my work at Saint Meinrad Seminary, I get to do all the things I love to do. I want to go out "with my alb on," not sitting around some old priests' home talking about how great things used to be. I don't want to be an 80-year-old priest with a past. I want to be an 80-year-old priest with a future.

Even though I have had a lot of help from God and many people, this has not happened by accident. I have worked hard to reject the notion that life is something that happens to you and all you can do is make the most of it. I believe that life isn't about finding yourself as much as it about creating yourself.

What I am trying to teach the seminarians at Saint Meinrad is, in the words of Pope John Paul II, "All formation, including priestly formation, is ultimately self-formation." All my priesthood, I have striven to be a force of nature, not some sniveling little clod of ailments and grievances complaining that the church will not get together and make me happy.

When it's over, I want to go out with a bang, not a whimper. I want to leap into the next life rather than go into it kicking and screaming.

Each of us will die someday, and our "professions," no matter what they are, will end. Over the last 38 years, I have tried to live the belief that the best thing for me to do is to live well each and every day. I don't want to put living off until some future time and then pathetically try to get ready to die at the last minute. The challenge for me is to be ready, to live with my bags packed, to milk life for all it's worth, knowing that all of this could be over before this day is done.

Anniversaries are about celebrating how far we have come, but they are also about taking stock of where we are going: correcting what needs to be corrected, ceasing to blame circumstances and people and answering our calls with even more fidelity.

The biggest tragedy of life is not dying, but getting to the end and realizing that we have not really lived or accomplished anything.

May 15, 2008

He who feeds on me will have life.
JOHN 6:57

This weekend we will celebrate the feast of the Body and Blood of Christ. I started thinking about this feast during Christmas.

What grabbed my attention last Christmas, as I read the very familiar story once more, was the word "manger." The word "manger" comes from a Latin word meaning "to eat."

Not only do we do a lot of eating in celebration of the Christmas holiday, it seems that the whole of Jesus was very much involved with eating and drinking. Therefore, it is not surprising that Jesus would come into this world and be placed right away in a "manger," a "feed box." Even the city in which he was born, Bethlehem, means "house of bread." In fact, the word "bread" is mentioned at least 300 times in the Bible.

The very first miracle that Jesus performed, the opening statement and symbol of his ministry, was the multiplication of wine at the marriage feast of Cana. The Jewish rabbis had a saying that "without wine, there is no joy." Jesus claimed in his teaching that he had come to bring life, and this miracle was a powerful, tangible symbol of that rich and full life.

In his public ministry, as a way to reach out to the lost sheep of this world, Jesus regularly welcomed sinners and ate with them. He did it so often that his enemies nicknamed him a "glutton and a drunkard" and a "friend of sinners."

One of his greatest miracles was what has been called the "multiplication of the loaves," where hundreds were fed from five of loaves of bread, with a whole lot left over.

Jesus often compared heaven to a wedding feast, at which the good and the bad alike will be invited to dine with God, a feast like the one Isaiah talked about. "On this mountain, God will set a table for all people, loaded down with pure choice wines and juicy, rich food."

Jesus compared his invisible "kingdom in our midst" to the bread-baking process when yeast slowly infects a mass of dough. It is already here, working almost imperceptibly.

In the Lord's Prayer, we are encouraged to ask for our "daily bread" from "Abba," an incredibly loving and generous God.

His last gift to us was a meal, the Eucharist, at which he is the host and the main course. He gives us himself, under the signs of bread and wine, and invites us to "feed on" him, taking on his strength, until he comes again.

In the Christmas Gospel, Jesus was called "Emmanuel," meaning God-with-us. On this feast, he will be "placed in the manger," on the altar, our "table of plenty," to be bread for our journey and strength for our trip as we continue this adventure that we call "life." Let us not fail to "feed on" him, as a community, while we can.

May 22, 2008

We hear them speaking in our own tongues
of the mighty acts of God.
ACTS 2:11

June is the traditional month when the clergy personnel boards "open the envelopes" and tell people whom their new priest is going to be.

In the old days of the 1970s and 1980s, the question people used to ask themselves was, "What kind of priest do you think we will get, a liberal or a conservative?" The question has changed dramatically in the last few years. Today, the question might be, "What kind of priest do you think we might get: Vietnamese, Nigerian, Indian or Filipino?"

It may shock some Catholics to know, especially in the middle of the country where we live, that at least 28 percent of all American priests serving our parishes today were born in another country.

It might shock some Catholics, as well, to know that this has almost always been true. The Catholic church in the United States has almost always depended on international priests to serve its parishes, with the notable exception of the 1940s and 1950s. That period, contrary to what most Catholics think, was an exception to the rule.

In 1791, when we were still part of the Diocese of Baltimore, eighty percent of the clergy were foreign-born.

In the years following the establishment of our diocese in Bardstown in 1808, our first three bishops were born in France.

My own parish, St. Theresa Church in Meade County, founded in 1818, was served in its earliest years by priests born in France, Belgium, Germany, Holland and Ireland.

By the time the present Cathedral of the Assumption was completed in 1852, 30 of the 47 American bishops were foreign born, and hordes of Irish and German priests entered our diocese to serve a burgeoning immigrant population.

Barring a miracle, the future picture of American Catholicism is most probably one of a shortage of American seminarians and an endless effort to recruit priests from overseas.

In my years as the vocation director for this archdiocese, I was happy to present for ordination priests from Vietnam, Puerto Rico, El Salvador and Zambia.

These days, I am working at Saint Meinrad Seminary, where we train young men born in places such as Vietnam, Mexico, India, South Korea, Kenya, Tanzania, Zambia, Columbia, Ecuador, the Bahamas, Nigeria, Togo and Switzerland to serve the national and international church.

This influx of new priests will challenge Catholics to see Catholicism in world terms, to learn about our own past and to develop better programs to welcome them to their new ministry here.

As much as we appreciate the help of these international priests, we must continue to ask our own American-born young men whether God is calling them to this ministry. We need both.

For all of you out there with unused frequent flyer miles on Delta or American that you would like to give away, I know some wonderful international seminarians always needing to visit their families back home: rknott@saintmeinrad.edu.

May 29, 2008

Teaching the Advantages of Good Behavior

One of the habits I have fallen into while living alone is having the TV on in the background as I work at the computer, even if I am not paying attention to what's on the television. I guess it is remote preparation for having my wheelchair parked in front of a TV in some nursing home someday.

The other day, Oprah was on in the background. That day, her show featured male and female guests with histories of marital cheating. I perked up in disgust, thinking that it was going to be another one of those shows that touted the advantages of such behavior, calling it "enlightened." I reached for the remote.

Before I could turn it off, I got hooked. Instead of each one of the guests bragging about how their "affairs" had enriched their lives, they told the audience, one by one, how destructive these affairs had been to their spouses and to them personally. They reflected on the personal dishonesty that enabled them to get involved and stay involved. Instead of glamorizing such behavior, the show was very effective in exposing the personal destruction of such choices. The guests that day made a great case for "thou shalt not commit adultery."

As I sat there engaged in the discussion, I could not help but think that if it had been a religious TV program, the focus would have been totally different. Typically, it would have featured an angry clergyman ranting about today's promiscuous culture and threatening damnation. With all heat and no light, nobody would have been converted, and even more people would have solidified their position that the church has nothing to say about such issues.

There are many in the church today who think that their only job is to name sin and condemn it. What we really need, I believe, is the ability to sell the advantages of good behavior and to convince people of the merits of virtuous living. As John Locke once said, "It is one thing to show a man that he is in error and another to put him in possession of the truth." I suppose that's all you can do if he is not very skillful as a spiritual leader.

My complaint today is not about what the church teaches, but about our inability to inspire people to accept what the church teaches. We have a lot to say, but we are pathetic sometimes is the way we say it.

We seem to be much more concerned about showing people their errors than putting them in possession of the truth. No wonder we have recently lost our place as the biggest Christian denomination in the United States to Evangelical Protestants.

Why do so many Catholics feel they have to leave the church to hear the Gospel? Maybe that's what happens when you preach what one former bishop called "churchianity" instead of the Gospel — the earthenware jar instead of the treasure.

June 5, 2008

While we were still sinners, Christ died for us.
ROMANS 5:8

Many people think they have to be perfect to be loved by God. They grew up on the bankrupt theology that says, "God loves us when we are good, quits loving us when we are bad and starts loving us again when we shape up." Underneath all that thinking is the belief that we earn our way into God's graces by good behavior. Nothing could be further from the truth.

The truth of the matter is, when we finally hear the "good news" and realize that we are loved by God, without condition, no "ands, ifs or buts about it," we are more likely to respond with good behavior. God never quits loving us. When we finally "get" that, we are ready to let him transform our lives.

I have always loved the words of the second Eucharistic Prayer for Reconciliation: "When we were lost and could not find our way to you, you loved us even more." That truth, of course, is the message of Jesus' Parable of the Lost Sheep. In that parable, God is the shepherd who goes out to look desperately for his lost sheep, and when he finds it, he puts it on his shoulders, carries it home, and calls his friends and neighbors together to celebrate.

That parable reminds me of a story told by Father Anthony DeMello. "God in heaven holds each person by a string. When you sin, you cut the string. Then God ties it up again, making a knot — and thereby bringing you a little closer to him. Again and again your sin cuts the string — and with each further knot God keeps drawing you closer and closer."

Many well-meaning religious teachers, scandalized by "people's behavior today," believe that the best way to insure personal change is to "put the fear of the Lord into them" by delivering a stinging message of "fire and brimstone." With all those doing that these days, you would think that by now, society would be making dramatic turns for the better.

What changes people's hearts is not fear and condemnation, but the love-message of the parables. The harsh, condemning message of the Pharisees drove people away from God. The unconditional love-message of the parables brought many people to Jesus and caused their lives to be transformed. They did not come to God out of fear, but out of love.

Several years back our church moved away from delivering a harsh, condemning religious message. Some people think that was a mistake — a mistake that gave people permission to do "whatever they pleased."

I happen to believe that the message of "unconditional love" is not a "mistake" that we ought to back away from. It is, rather, our core message. The "mistake" would be giving up on the central Christian message of God's unconditional love and replacing it with obsessing on liturgical minutiae, intra-church legalisms and other secondary concerns.

June 12, 2008

THERE IS MORE AGREEMENT THAN DISAGREEMENT

Several have made the claim that the Catholic church in America is polarized and beset my acrimony and suspicion, with conservatives regularly accusing liberals of heresy and liberals charging conservatives with abandoning basic Gospel values.

Having the advantage of moving through several seminaries, presbyterates and parishes, I believe that this may be more true of church professionals than of people in the pew.

Social scientists tell us that there are many reasons why dedicated and well-motivated members of a group turn their frustrations on one another. Changes that are unforeseen, ill prepared-for and overwhelming will produce anxiety in the community, and its members will try to manage that anxiety by primitive processes of scapegoating and projection.

Facing difficult changes, the group will psychologically split itself into the "good guys" and the "bad guys," those who are "orthodox" and those who are not. These ideological splits take on a life of their own, with participants believing that they are fighting a battle over beliefs and values.

While members of the group actually agree more than they disagree, these skirmishes serve as containers for the group's anxiety. They become chronic defense mechanisms when group members fail to recognize the true source of their anxiety: how difficult their professional lives have become and how uneasy they feel about their effectiveness.

With so many dramatic changes in ministerial partnerships (largely with women), priorities (beyond the confines of its early immigrant history), world views and perceptions (the religious needs of an increasingly more complex and diversified spectrum of Catholic cultures and communities), no wonder people are tempted to look for scapegoats on which to blame it all.

These dynamics are true not only in the church, but also in American politics. In fact, we have, in the church, adopted much of the demonizing language of political talk shows.

With so much social complexity in our culture, "nativists" blame immigrants, "conservatives" blame "liberals" and "liberals" blame "conservatives" for everything they feel is going wrong. Other favorite scapegoats include gays and welfare recipients.

How do we change this direction, in our church and in our country? Unfortunately, there is no easy solution no matter how many are put forward. The way forward is tough, but solutions are possible if we are willing to work for them, one person at a time.

We must gain clarity on what is truly essential and what is not. We must avoid arrogance, barbed words and bitterness in our talk. We must strive for individual patience with contradiction and for an inclination toward generosity of spirit. We must reach toward acceptance of the fact that divergent views often serve to complete each other.

We must be ready to let go of our attachment to our own preferences and points of view. We must engage in broader consultation and accept co-responsibility for directions taken and choices to be made. Finally, we must accept workable and reasonable structures for the sake of unity, even if they are not perfect.

June 19, 2008

Today, I set before you life and death. Choose life!
DEUTERONOMY 30:19

Trash TV is forever giving some of the weakest people in our culture a place to show off their ignorance. I must confess that I get sucked into watching it sometimes — usually with a jaw dropped in amazement. Just when you think you've heard and seen it all, the ante is usually upped in one form or another.

One of the themes that gets regular coverage is the inability to say "no." Pathetic examples of humanity tell the audience in a million different ways that if the temptation is there, one is forced to act on it because one is totally powerless to do otherwise. Likewise, if the opportunity arises to commit adultery, defraud the government or take something from work, we are told that a person would be foolish to pass it up.

A person of integrity knows right from wrong and has the strength of character to choose what is right — even when no one is looking and even when it is possible to choose what is wrong and get away with it. The opposite of a person with integrity is a small, self-centered person, always on the make. If you are interested in bucking this trend and becoming a person of integrity, let me share a few thoughts with you from a new favorite book called *Virtuous Leadership: An Agenda for Personal Excellence.*

The ability to say "no" to opportunistic situations is one of the most basic abilities of a person of integrity. A person of integrity declares his independence from the terminal egoism of popular culture. He responds to life from well-defined principles, not the basest of addictions.

A person of integrity says "no" to the cynicism that says the end justifies the means. When we buy into the latter perspective, we are willing to use deception, manipulation and even death to accomplish our "good" goals. Consider Lenin, Hitler and Mao, who killed millions of innocent people in the name of an ideology, and then consider much of the pro-abortion and assisted-suicide rhetoric.

A person of integrity says "no" to materialism — that driving passion to "own," "possess" and "have" at any cost, even at the expense of individuals and communities. Such a person sees others simply as cogs in a machine, devoid of spirituality and transcendent value.

A person of integrity says "no" to radical individualism. Radical individualists focus on serving themselves, always taking and never giving back. We are social beings by nature. We live in communities and are therefore never free in an absolute sense.

A person of integrity says "no" to the "group-think" and what "everybody else is doing" that makes it impossible to love what is best in one's self. Unable to love themselves, they are unable to love others. Unable to love others, they cannot sustain life within the family and, in fact, find family life stultifying.

If all this sounds terribly counter-cultural, it is.

June 26, 2008

With Rights Ought to Come Responsibilities

Everyone should bear his own responsibility.
GALATIANS 6:5

Tomorrow we will celebrate our political independence from England. The Declaration of Independence is our country's birth certificate.

This unanimous declaration of the 13 United States of America, signed July 4, 1776, stated that, "We hold these truths to be self-evident, that all men are created equal, that they are endowed by their Creator with certain unalienable rights, that among these are life, liberty and the pursuit of happiness."

A couple of years after the Constitution of the United Sates was ratified on Sept. 17, 1787, James Madison introduced his proposed amendments to that Constitution. These amendments would eventually become known as the Bill of Rights, guaranteeing specific rights and liberties omitted in the crafting of the original Constitution. Because of our founders' own experiences, they were very concerned about personal rights.

Our founders failed to balance this "bill of rights" with a "bill of responsibilities." They probably did not think it necessary because they lived in the days of closely-knit communities and religiously committed individuals when an individual's responsibilities were clear and obvious to everyone.

Two hundred twenty-two years later, it is clear and obvious to almost everyone that things have changed drastically. Rights are taken for granted while responsibilities are shirked. In a recent study, when a sampling of young Americans were asked what was so special about the United States, they responded, "Individualism and the fact that you can do whatever you want."

It is obvious that when responsibilities are separated from rights, that kind of thinking becomes common. The behaviors that flow from that kind of thinking follow quickly and begin to eat away at our social and moral fabric.

In a 1992 study, when the problems of high school teachers of today were compared to the problems of high school teachers of the 1940s, teachers in the 1940s listed the top five problems as: talking out of turn, making noise, cutting in line, littering and chewing. In today, the top five problems facing teachers are: drug abuse, alcohol use, pregnancy, suicide and rape.

Some have suggested that we convene another constitutional convention to draft a corresponding "bill of responsibilities." Among some of the suggestions that have been made are: voting, serving on a jury, resolving conflicts through mediation and arbitration, maintaining a sense of stewardship of the environment and volunteering for service of some kind by all.

For many of us the Ten Commandments serve as a "bill of responsibilities," but they actually are considered religious commandments. Because of that, maybe another constitutional convention could say many of the same things in a "legal" way.

Because these responsibilities are ultimately inner commitments, these values cannot be recovered by passing new laws. They must be individually chosen, and it is the job of the church to call, in a more convincing way than we have been doing, for such conversion of life. As long as we fail to motivate, there will be pressure to legislate.

July 3, 2008

The "Mother Church" Is All-Embracing

They were all in one place together.
ACTS 2:1

Recently, while reading an intriguing article in the Spring 2008 issue of CHURCH magazine entitled "Quirky Catholic Reality" by Lawrence Cunningham, I experienced a flashback to my mother when I was a kid.

My mother loved her kids, not just in some figurative sense, but also in a tangible, hands-on kind of way. I can remember one day when we were all horsing around with her. She ended up hugging all six of us in her lap at one time. It is one of those very special memories from my childhood that makes me smile every time I remember it.

Mother church also has long arms and a big lap where she can hug a lot of marvelous reality at the same time.

Do you like exuberance? Join a charismatic prayer group or attend Mass at a local African-American parish. Are you partial to silence? Make a retreat with the Trappists. Do you have strong views on peace and social justice issues? Start a Catholic Worker House or join one.

Want to be a nun? There are about 500 different communities in this country eager for candidates. Crazy about devotions? Hop on a plane to Medjugorje or go visit Mother Angelica's place down in Irondale, Alabama. Enamored with the Bible? Join one of hundreds of local Bible study groups. Parishes routinely advertise a variety of devotional exercises — an expansive menu of diverse styles of devotional exercises and spiritual practices — be they the exercises of Third Order members, Taize prayer, Eucharistic adoration, centering prayer or meditation groups.

Walking into a traditional Catholic church is like walking through an archeological display from the ages: altars and ambos from ancient times; side altars from the Romanesque period; stained-glass windows from the early medieval period; organs and choir lofts from the late medieval period through the Renaissance; Stations of the Cross from the 18th century; tabernacles on the main altar from the late medieval period and, in front of it, a table-altar from the Vatican II period.

Read a Catholic directory and see long lists of institutions such as schools, hospitals, orphanages, homeless shelters, programs for youth, feeding centers and homes for the elderly.

Catholic worship embraces a host of ordinary and extraordinary things such as candles, water, incense, organs, guitars, paintings, statues, oil, bread, wine, elaborate vestments and simple cloth, words and gestures, stained glass, palms, ashes and fire.

Mother church has long arms and a big lap. At a gathering of the Catholic church, such as the funeral of a pope, you realize that we are not some newly-founded, suburban church where everybody looks like everybody else. When we get together, you will see people of every culture and skin color on the face of the globe.

I don't know about you, but I like being hugged by Mother church in a lap full of people from every time, place and culture on earth.

July 10, 2008

Anticipate one another in showing honor.
ROMANS 12:10

At a meeting I attended last fall, the Rev. Kevin Cosby affirmed something that I have come to believe in deeply. He said, "Before you can correct, you have to connect."

This is something I learned the hard way. At Saint Thomas, the former minor seminary here in Louisville, the thinking was that we were terribly flawed young men, and the job of the staff was to look for those flaws and drill them out like a dentist would a cavity. Of course, I had many such "cavities" to be drilled. I coped by hiding my "cavities" from their sight.

When I arrived at Saint Meinrad Seminary for the second half of my training, they took a different tack. They told us that we all had gifts and talents that they wanted to identify and help "grow." Of course, I had some, but they were deeply buried, even from my own sight. Over the years, and to my own amazement, they dug them out like rough diamonds and helped me polish them.

To this day, I have little patience with "religious types" who are always "mousing for vermin," always looking for sins to condemn rather than virtues to affirm.

My last class each spring for those about to be ordained priests is always one on "the spiritual art of blessing people." I try to teach them what Rev. Cosby put into those colorful words, "Before you can correct, you must connect."

The spiritual art of blessing people is, of course, about more than waving crosses over them. It is about looking for goodness to affirm, rather than evil to name, as the better path to spiritual leadership.

We live in a mean world, and priests are not immune from it. The caustic, harsh, strident, biting, stinging, scathing, cutting and nasty words come too easily to our lips. We have the "talk shows" to thank for this. Political pundits are the worst. They have taught us that when we disagree with someone, we have the right to label them with whatever vicious words we can find. Many in the church have picked up on this meanness, especially in ideological "blogs" on the Internet. Even little kids are doing it.

"Every snowflake in an avalanche pleads not guilty." It is the accumulation of this meanness that is doing tremendous damage to church and country.

What is the antidote for this meanness? I believe the best way to spiritual transformation is the "spiritual practice of blessing people," looking for goodness to affirm and not just badness to condemn.

Some find it nearly impossible to come right out and give a clear compliment. Henry Ward Beecher once said, "The meanest, most contemptible kind of praise is that which first speaks well of a man, and then qualifies it with a "but."

I believe Albert Schweitzer had a better idea. "Constant kindness can accomplish much. As the sun makes ice melt, kindness causes misunderstanding, mistrust and hostility to evaporate."

July 17, 2008

The rains fell, the floods came and the winds blew …
but it did not collapse; it had been set solidly on rock.
MATTHEW 7:25

Maybe I should have been an architect, because I have a soft spot in my heart for old buildings. I have some of the same feelings for them that I have for neglected old people from whom love and care have been withdrawn.

When I see old buildings along some street or roadway, it is not uncommon for me to "fix them up in my mind," to imagine how they would look all painted and rehabilitated.

Before it got to be too time-consuming and expensive, I did "adopt" some of these "orphaned" buildings. I have restored or remodeled at least five old houses. The latest was an 1867 farmhouse in Meade County. Each one of them whispered secrets to me about the lives of the people who lived in them before they were abandoned.

Neglected old buildings make me profoundly sad, especially old churches. I have had a hand in renovating, restoring or revitalizing at least two old churches — Holy Name of Mary in Calvary (built 1891-1895) and the Cathedral of the Assumption (built 1849-1852). The very boards dripped with the prayers and smelled of incense.

There are hundreds and hundreds of these beautiful old churches in almost every city in this country — beautiful, finely crafted, architectural jewels. Sadly, some have been abandoned or left to decay and vandalism. Nobody can afford to build them like that any more, and nobody has figured out yet how to move them. Having died or moved elsewhere, the faith crawled out of them many years ago and now they stand there, empty shells of bygone glory.

Sadder still are those glorious old churches in Europe. People would die to protect these old buildings, but no one seems willing to die for the faith that used to live and was celebrated within them. That faith seems to have evaporated, except in the hearts of a few old women. They are now museums of former belief.

We use the word "church" interchangeably. Sometimes we mean those buildings where people of faith gather, and sometimes we mean the people of faith gathered in those buildings. The "church" as a building is obviously not the same as the "church" as a people. They are, however, deeply connected. You can tell a lot about the "church" by looking at its "churches."

When I was a vocation director, I used to travel around the diocese almost every weekend visiting parishes to talk about vocations. I could almost always tell the level of faith by the way they kept their churches.

I still remember the vibrant faith of Holy Trinity in Springfield with its immaculately kept property. I can also remember another recently closed church, not that old, that had lots of grass growing in the cracks of its sidewalks and overcrowding its flower beds. In both cases, the inside reflected the outside.

July 24, 2008

*Those parts of the body that we consider less
honorable we surround with greater honor.*
1 CORINTHIANS 12:23

Last week, I talked about church buildings, especially those grand old structures built in hard times by people whose faith was intense.

They felt that they were building a house for God, and so they put everything they had into their work. The buildings are impressive, but the faith behind these monumental structures is even more impressive. We are more ambivalent toward God these days, and our buildings reflect it.

This week, I would like to say something about those of us who make up the church as a living body — a body with that ancient faith still running through our veins. I would also like to say something about the church as an institution. I will then have talked about the "church" as a building, as a people and as an institution.

We need buildings, and we need organizational structures, but in the strictest sense of the word we are the church. Through us, his body, Jesus is active in the world today. We are his ambassadors. We are the earthenware jar that holds his great treasure.

One of my favorite new quotes about us being the church is one by James H. Aughey when he says: "The church is not a select circle of the immaculate, but a home where the outcast may come in. It is not a palace with gate attendants and challenging sentinels along the entrance-ways holding off at arm's length the stranger, but rather a hospital where the broken-hearted may be healed and where all the weary and troubled may find rest and take counsel together."

This seems to be Jesus' vision of the church in the Gospel. "I have come to seek out and save what was lost." "The healthy do not need the doctor. Sick people do." "Go out into the highways and byways and bring as many as you can in." "This man welcomes sinners and eats with them." "The good shepherd leaves the ninety-nine and goes out looking for the lost sheep." "Come to me, all you who are weary and find life burdensome, and I will refresh you."

When the church is overcome with fear, the gate-keepers tend to hold the marginal and those who have failed at bay, doling out God's mercy in thimbles as if there were a shortage.

Because of the nature of our training for ministry, we gate-keepers tend to define ourselves in relationship to the institution, thus keeping institutional needs central in our lives. We can sometimes become preoccupied with keeping sinners at arm's length and tending to the ninety-nine.

The people we are called to serve have a different agenda. They are typically preoccupied with things such as birth, death, sickness, financial survival, arguing and reconciling, hospitality and farewells. They look to the church leadership for comfort, hope, healing and meaning. They know they have failed. They just want to be assured that they are loved.

July 31, 2008

93

He shouted even louder, "I want to see!"
LUKE 18:41

I like this Bartimeus, this blind man in the scripture passage quoted above. He is a man who knows what he wants, and he is out to get what he wants. No wimp is he, sitting back and wishing and waiting for what he needs. He is willing to do whatever it takes to get what he needs!

No hoping to be noticed here – he makes sure he is noticed. Nobody's "sit down and shut up" will stop him. This man desperately wants to see. With his burning faith in Jesus, he will not be held back by anybody.

It is important to notice the exact words of Jesus here. Jesus does not say, "Go! My faith has healed you!" Instead he says, "Go! Your faith has healed you!" In fact, there are failed healing stories in the gospel where Jesus could not work any miracle "because of their lack of faith."

The one necessary ingredient, then, in all healing miracles is a strong belief that healing is possible. This strong belief triggers an abnormal acceleration of natural healing processes. This is true of the healing shrines in all religions – it is the strong belief that sets healing powers into action!

Very often we are ambivalent about what we say we want. We say we want things to be different, but in reality, we are not so sure. We often do not want things to change all that much.

Any other blind man might have said that he wanted to see, but in reality he might not, because seeing again would require that he give up begging and get a job. Some people wallow in grief for years over the loss of a spouse, unable to move forward. They say they would like to get over it, but in reality, they are scared of having to do the work of building a new life – a scary new life of their own. It's safer to stay stuck!

Miracles are possible in our lives. However, we can't just sit around and wish. We must get up and make things happen. "I wish I could lose weight!" "I wish I could find a job!" Like Bartimeus, we have to get up, throw away whatever excuses we have wrapped ourselves in, ask for what we need and override the nay-sayer in ourselves and among our friends. Wishing waits for others to fix us. Really wanting something makes us take action!

Friends, we can begin to work miracles in our own lives by really wanting and believing that what we need is possible. As Dale Carnegie once wrote, "Believe that you will succeed … believe it firmly and you will do what is necessary to bring it to success."

"By believing passionately in that which does exist, we create it. That which is nonexistent has not been sufficiently desired." (Nikos Kazantzakis) "Whatever you ask for in prayer with faith, you will receive." (Matthew 21:22)

August 7, 2008

These you should have done,
without neglecting the others.
MATTHEW 23:23

The incredible story of Irena Sendler, 98, who died in Poland back in May, didn't make the daily paper, even though she was a real-life hero. It was not to be found among all the stories about Brittany Spears and some politician's latest sex scandal. The news sees us human beings as half empty, and so covers only the twisted and sick. Sadly, it sells!

Who was Irena Sendler? She was a Catholic social worker who risked her life during World War II to smuggle 2,500 Jewish children from the Warsaw Ghetto, saving them from the ravages of the Holocaust. She smuggled them in boxes, suitcases or hidden in trolleys and gave them new identities. Pope John XXIII, then Cardinal Roncalli, did the same thing in Turkey for Jewish children by forging baptismal certificates so as to help them escape the Nazis.

A Catholic woman risking her life for Jewish children at a time when millions wouldn't! She was arrested and tortured by the Gestapo. She only escaped execution when some friends managed to bribe some Nazi officials, who left her in the woods unconscious but alive with broken legs and arms.

I read her story right after someone told me that a bunch of people had stopped going to their parishes because Archbishop Kurtz is insisting that we follow the liturgical changes mandated by Rome. What a contrast! One Catholic willing to die to save Jewish children and other Catholics willing to drop out of their church because of a few liturgical changes! I am sure they are upset, but isn't it obvious that when we take those kinds of steps, we need to get a life?

While I personally do not see these liturgical practices as necessary or a great improvement, I refuse to get twisted out of shape about them. At Bellarmine, we just made the changes and moved on! As a young priest, this would have been a live-or-die battle, but now I would rather spend my energy on something more important.

Both mandating liturgical minutiae and resisting liturgical minutiae are focused on the earthenware jar instead of the treasure contained therein. I can connect with God standing, and I can connect with God kneeling. Resisting either is a waste of time in my book. Since we pray as a community and not as individuals at the Eucharist, group norms are necessary. The church is not asking us to lay down our lives here! In communal worship, in contrast to individual prayer, liturgical norms are important, so let's just do it and get on with more important things!

All this is important, but not that important. We need to call people to something greater than liturgical conformity, participating in parish pot lucks or even volunteering for a unpaid ministry position at a weekend Mass. We need more Irena Sendlers, people who are willing to put their lives on the line for their faith.

August 14, 2008

Balancing Communality and Individuality

I have lived through a great shift in our culture. I have lived long enough to see ga pendulum swing between an over-emphasis on the good of the community to the expense of individuals, to an over-emphasis on the good of individuals to the expense of the community.

This shift has taken place in the church as well. When I was a child, the church emphasized the good of the community sometimes to the detriment of individuals. The authority of the institution, not the authority of the individual, was the law of the land. We did as we were told. Communality thrived, while individuality suffered!

Five years before I was ordained, 1966 to be precise, the church started changing very quickly. All that individuality that had been held down and held back for centuries, by the church and by the culture, came roaring out. We said to ourselves, "Do your own thing! Follow your own conscience! Decide for yourself!"

The phrase "pro-choice" epitomizes just how far this cultural change has gone. Individual authority, not institutional authority, has become the prevailing wisdom. "I'll do as I please!" is a popular principle that many follow, sometimes without many boundaries and often without much thought. Individual rights are valued. Communal values are kicked to the curb.

Now that we have run off both sides of the road, maybe it is time to make a correction – something in the center – where the values of community and the values of individuality can both be valued and honored.

For three years, I have been flying around the country talking to groups of priests about this very issue. Before my time, priesthood was so standardized for the sake of unity that individuality in the priesthood was for all practical purposes impossible. After Vatican II, when individual priests were given air to breathe, we became known as "Lone Rangers" or "priests in private practice."

What I try to promote in these priest gatherings is a balance between individuality and community. For the sake of a coherent and high-quality service to the People of God, we must be willing to move from our personal points of view to a communal viewing point. From there we can appreciate not just our own perspective, but also those of others. That honors both our individuality as well as our communality!

This struggle is the struggle of our church today: balancing communality and individuality, being one and being catholic, maintaining our unity while being as inclusive as possible – all this without running off either side of the road. Heresy, as some have said, is simply the truth grossly exaggerated.

This balance of communality and individuality is a need not only in our church, but also in our culture. Alexis de Tocqueville identified "a shared sense of community – the willingness to recognize that there is a greater good above ourselves as individuals – as a key factor in our nation's rise to greatness."

August 21, 2008

Prosper the work of our hands for us!
PSALM 90:17

Next week, we celebrate Labor Day. This day is more than just a nondescript national holiday into which many of us in this country have very little insight. It should be a reminder of how far workers have come in this country.

Labor Day, the first Monday in September, is a creation of the labor movement and is dedicated to the social and economic achievements of American workers. It constitutes a yearly, national tribute to the contributions workers have made to the strength, prosperity and well-being of our country.

The first Labor Day holiday was organized on Tuesday, September 5, 1882, in New York City by the Central Labor Union. It spread to other states until June 28, 1894, when Congress passed an act making it a legal holiday on the first Monday in September of each year.

It was only four years later, in 1891, that Pope Leo XIII, "the workers' Pope," issued his famous encyclical, *Rerum Novarum*, in which some basic moral principles on human labor, which we take for granted today, were promulgated by the church. They include the natural right to the ownership of private property; the right of workers to form trade unions and of employers to form parallel organizations; the right to an adequate period of rest, recreation, safe and hygienic work conditions; the right to a just wage and the right to religious freedom.

Since then several Popes, especially John Paul II, have applied those principles to a post-cold war and highly technological age.

My own eyes were opened to just how bad the labor situation was during the time Pope Leo XIII was drafting his Rerum Novarum when we were remodeling the cathedral undercroft. Traces of the kindergarten and night school for "bootblacks," newsboys and children working in factories and shops, founded by ladies of the parishes in 1889, were still there. There were, at one time, 125 working boys and girls, ages 8 to 24, attending night school in that basement. This basement night school of child-workers included a gym and a recreation hall.

Let me end this column with four quotes – one on hard work, another on humble work, another on the responsibility of work and one on enjoyable work.

"Opportunity is missed by most because it is dressed in overalls and looks like work." Thomas A. Edison

"I long to accomplish great and noble tasks, but it is my chief duty to accomplish humble tasks as though they were great and noble. The world is moved along not only by the mighty shoves of its heroes, but also by the aggregate of the tiny pushes of each honest worker." Helen Keller

"Work while you have the light. You are responsible for the talent that has been entrusted to you." Henri F. Amiel

"The secret of joy in work is contained in one word – excellence. To know how to do something well is to enjoy it." Pearl Buck

August 28, 2008

While we were still sinners, Christ died for us.
ROMANS 5:8

One of the biggest mistakes people make when it comes to religion – on both sides of the pulpit – is the belief that people have to get their lives together before they can come to God. The truth of the matter is that once we give our messy and broken lives to God, our lives come together.

Some church people, especially of the gate-keeper variety, spend a lot of time and energy making sure that sinners and other law-breakers are restricted from the loving embrace of the church lest they contaminate the saved and muddle the message. As a result, many have their path to sainthood blocked because they never get close enough to God to be transformed by his loving embrace.

Because of these exclusionary methods, all in the name of purity of religion, many people believe that God is exclusionary as well. The truth of the matter is that Christ did his dying for us while we were sinners, not as a reward to be bestowed after we have repented. Sadly we all grow to resemble the God we believe in – whether the God we believe in is stingy or lavish with his love!

Because of my own path to God and own struggle with being "good enough," I have always taken great comfort in passages like these: "Come to me all you who are weary and find life burdensome and I will refresh you," "This man welcomes sinners and eats with them," "… the parts of the body that we consider less honorable we surround with greater honor, and the less presentable parts are treated with greater propriety…" and "We love because he first loved us."

Because of their transforming power, these words have compelled me to risk sharing my struggles with not being "good enough" with the readers of this column and others. By doing so, I have found out yet again that when others have been able to bring their broken and messy lives to God, they too have seen their lives come together.

When the gospel is preached – the basic good news that we are loved without condition – with passion and clarity and without equivocation, transformation happens. God sees to it. The church needs structures and rules, but the more convincingly the gospel is preached, the less structures and rules are needed. But if the basic gospel is neglected, if secondary issues become the primary focus, those structures and rules become irrelevant when more and more people withdraw their consent to be guided by the church.

We must bring people to God no matter what their condition and resist efforts to demand that they be "acceptable" before we allow them to bask in the presence of God. God is not diminished by their sins. He died for those sins. It is in bringing our messy lives to God that they come together. When we can't "get it together," God can "put us together."

September 4, 2008

Whichever he chooses shall be given him.
SIRACH 15:17

One of the most life-changing books I ever read was Victor Frankl's "Man's Search for Meaning." As has been the case with other books, God seems to have put that book on my path at a time when I needed it.

One passage that affected me deeply was this one: "Everything can be taken from a man but one thing – the last of the human freedoms – to choose one's attitude in any given set of circumstances – to choose one's own response."

You can make the future better by choosing your response to it. I certainly did not want to go to southern Kentucky for my first assignment as a priest. I tried to get it changed to no avail. I felt very powerless. Halfway there I made a conscious decision to "go with it," to try to make it the best assignment I could. Because I chose to respond positively in that present moment, the future turned out to be a very positive experience.

To those who say you cannot change the past, I say "rubbish!" You can change the past by re-choosing how you want to remember the events that took place there. Memories can be healed. I can still remember the very day that I chose how I wanted to react to a long held and bothersome parental resentment. One night I consciously decided to re-choose – to respond differently. Because I chose to respond differently to those past events, our relationship became different for both of us as we moved into the future. Choosing one's response can bring freedom!

As a priest, I meet so many people who have not yet discovered this freedom. They carry around big bags of stinking garbage in the backs of their minds. They really don't carry them as much as hug them! As another Sirach passage (27:30) says, "Wrath and anger are hateful things, yet the sinner hugs them tight." They have the twisted thinking that says, "I'll get you! I'll hurt me!"

What is some of the "garbage" that people continue to hug? It can be as simple as a flippant remark that someone made in the heat of an argument or as serious as a careless accident that led to significant property damage. It can be as sad as the loss of a loved one or as silly as the loss of a piece of cheap jewelry. Some of us hang onto that cutting remark, that damaged property, that missing loved one or that lost jewelry for years and years and years – as well as the mental pain and constant retelling of the loss that goes with it. We all have some of these things filed away in our minds that keep bringing us pain.

Our first response does not have to be a life response. Truly, the last great freedom is the ability to choose one's attitude in any set of circumstances – to choose (or re-choose) one's own response. Re-choose and be free!

September 11, 2008

Promote the welfare of the city.
For upon its welfare depends your own.
JEREMIAH 29:7

I love to collect the wise words of the world's spiritual leaders. I am always copying, clipping and pasting these quotes into journals for further reflection or possible use in this column.

The other day, I came upon a quote from Mahandas Gandhi, spiritual leader and the father of India's independence. It is called the "Roots of Violence." He lists seven sources of violence. He nails our culture with precision. I would like to share those seven "roots" and comment on them.

Wealth Without Work – Every state has got to have a lottery these days. However, many lottery winners will tell you that winning was the worst thing that happened to them. Many claim to have lost their friends and family due to large winnings and the circumstances that surround their new status in life. As George Bernard Shaw put it, "A perpetual holiday is a good working definition of hell."

Pleasure Without Conscience – Sexual boundaries are almost non-existent in many parts of our culture. Sexually transmitted diseases and routine abortions are considered "normal." Likewise, as a nation, we are eating ourselves to death. We cannot say "no" to our daily ration of "quarter-pounders with cheese" and "biggie fries" or, like huge hummingbirds, perpetually sipping on 32-oz. to-go cups, each with a zillion calories.

Knowledge Without Character – We have a whole lot of "smart" people who are willing to sell what they know to the highest bidder for self-aggrandizement. More slick than smart, they usually self-destruct after hurting a whole lot of people.

Commerce Without Morality – It is all too common to hear about how the crooked maneuvers of corporate leadership have ruined the lives of employees and retirees. Ill-gotten gains – scamming the poor, taking advantage of minorities, petty theft or embezzlement – are the same sins in different clothes.

Science Without Humanity – In the world of science, we have more "know-how" than "know why" sometimes. Should we do it just because we can do it? Who decides? How does one talk people out of crossing the line on things like human cloning and human-animal genetics?

Worship Without Sacrifice – We are much too self-absorbed in the church these days. We know we are in trouble when the battle over kneeling and standing becomes more important than the battle over ending the war, the lack of health care and the effect of the recession on poor families. It does take one's mind off the real issues facing the church – like our hemorrhaging of members to the evangelicals and a general denial of a looming shortage of clergy.

Politics Without Principles – The win-at-all-costs, character assassinating, influence-buying and dialing-for-dollars political campaigns will keep going till we pull the plug. They do it because it works and we pay for it!

These separations, according to Gandhi, cause violence in families, communities and nations. When we try to have one without the other, we end up with neither.

September 18, 2008